THE SPRING KING

THE SPRING KING

A Champion's Journey of Passion, Persistence, and Unlimited Possibility

Luis Perez

Published by Game Changer Publishing

Paperback ISBN: 978-1-966659-98-3

Hardcover ISBN: 978-1-966659-99-0

Digital ISBN: 978-1-967424-00-9

GC GAME CHANGER PUBLISHING

www.GameChangerPublishing.com

DEDICATION

To my wife, whose love, sacrifice, and unwavering belief in me have been my greatest source of strength.

To my daughters, who inspire me to be the best version of myself every day, I hope this story teaches you that no dream is too big and no obstacle is too great.

To my parents, who worked tirelessly to give me the opportunity to chase my dreams and who taught me that success is built on faith, discipline, and resilience.

To my coaches, teammates, and mentors who challenged me, pushed me, and believed in me when the odds said otherwise.

And to the dreamers, the underdogs, and the ones who refuse to quit—this book is for you. May my journey remind you that success isn't about where you start, but how far you're willing to go.

READ THIS FIRST

Just as a thank you for purchasing my book—I'd like to give you a free bonus gift, no strings attached. Enjoy!

Scan the QR Code Here:

THE SPRING KING

A CHAMPION'S JOURNEY OF PASSION,
PERSISTENCE, AND UNLIMITED POSSIBILITY

LUIS PEREZ

FOREWORD

BY COACH BOB STOOPS

The Spring King is an extraordinary story of perseverance, self-discipline, and the relentless pursuit of excellence. Luis Perez didn't grow up playing football, yet through sheer determination, he not only learned the game—he mastered it. His journey from teaching himself the sport to playing at a professional level is nothing short of remarkable. From college football to the XFL, UFL, and ultimately making it onto the Chargers' roster last summer—right up to the final cuts—his path is a testament to his resilience and unwavering belief.

Luis is the kind of athlete every coach wants on their team. He's a leader in every sense of the word, with an unshakable work ethic and a drive that sets him apart. His success is no accident—it's the result of many years of dedication, discipline, and an unrelenting commitment to professional growth.

I first met Luis through our personnel director, Rick Mueller, who recognized his talent and brought him in while I was coaching the Arlington Renegades. From the moment I saw him on the field, it was clear that Luis wasn't just another quarterback—he was a student of the game, a competitor who understood football at a level far beyond his experience. What he has achieved is almost unheard of.

In all my years in football, I can't recall another player who has accomplished what he has without a traditional football upbringing. His ability to adapt, lead, and execute under pressure speaks volumes about his character and his natural talent.

But Luis's skills aren't confined to the football field. Many might not know that he's also an exceptional bowler, having bowled ten or twelve perfect games—an accomplishment that requires incredible precision, discipline, and mental toughness. He's even considered going pro in bowling someday after he is done playing football, and honestly, I wouldn't bet against him. That's just who Luis is— someone who commits fully and excels at whatever he sets his mind to.

More than anything, what stands out about Luis is his resilience. Time and again, he has faced challenges that would have discour- aged most, yet he has never let setbacks define him. He stays the course, always pushing forward, always believing. And through it all, he remains humble, positive, and deeply respected by his teammates and coaches alike. He has an undeniable presence that lifts up those around him, both on and off the field.

Luis came incredibly close with the Chargers last year, and his journey is far from over. He remains steadfast in his dedication to the game, and with his relentless determination, success is inevitable.

The Spring King has only deepened my admiration for Luis. His story is inspiring, and his relentless drive is something we can all learn from. I have no doubt that readers will walk away just as inspired after reading this book.

– Coach Bob Stoops
National Championship (2000)
Winningest Coach in Oklahoma History (190 wins)
Inducted into the College Football Hall of Fame (2021)

CONTENTS

INTRODUCTION

My name is Luis Perez. I'm just a young guy who grew up in San Diego, California, with big dreams and aspirations.

I grew up with both parents and have two younger brothers. I loved football at a very young age and had a passion to do something with that. However, I had some ups and downs along the way.

I learned that the biggest thing is to get up when you're down and don't stay down too long. I wrote this book to show people that it doesn't matter what comes your way; it's how quickly you can get off that ground and continue to turn the page and move forward. This book is for anyone who feels like they can't get over the hump and break through to what they're trying to achieve. In it, I'm going to talk about everything I went through, from rock bottom to the peak of Mount Everest—and back down again because these peaks and troughs don't just happen once or twice; they happen a lot more.

Success rests on the way you shift your mindset, change your perspective on life, and create a better version of yourself. You should listen to me because I've done it. I've been through it for the last 20 years, since I was ten. It's been up and down every single year.

There's a lot to learn from my story and apply in your life.

Resiliency, determination, perseverance, work ethic, and passion for something—these things can take you over the top. Whatever you do in your life, you should do it 100%. Don't be a "one foot in, one foot out" type of person.

I hope that after reading this book, you will apply the lessons within to become a better human, overcome the obstacles in your path, and enjoy life more fully.

Everything is based on mindset and perspective. Nobody can do it on their own. You have to have a support system.

Everything has a positive. If you can start finding the positives in negative situations, your life will become a lot easier, you'll be able to get through obstacles much easier, and your mental state will be a lot better.

In this book, I'm going to talk about my childhood dream and how, at a young age, I had a vision. I pursued my dream with passion, resiliency, and tunnel vision, determined never to let anyone stop me.

I want everybody to know that every single goal we set for ourselves is within reach. If you have a plan for reaching your dream, no dream is too big.

We all have dreams, and I encourage you to pursue yours whole-heartedly. But pursuing a dream requires more than just desire—it demands a calculated approach and an unshakable belief that no obstacle can stand in your way. You must be willing to say, "No matter what happens, I will find a way to make this happen."

If you want something badly enough, you will find a way. And if you don't, perhaps you didn't want it enough to begin with.

ONE
BEGINNINGS OF A DREAM

I grew up in an athletic household. My dad was a professional soccer player, and my mom was a ballet dancer. I loved being outside. I was one of those kids who liked to be outside all day long. I did not want to do anything else.

I always had a football in my hand—I even slept with it. I took it to the store, brought it everywhere it was allowed, and even where it wasn't. There was just something about the pigskin that I fell in love with.

I vividly remember the love I had for that football and the comfort it gave me as a kid. I grew up a Chargers fan—the LaDainian Tomlinson, Antonio Gates, Vincent Jackson, and Drew Brees era. I just loved football.

I always had a vision of playing football as a kid. While playing in the backyard, my brothers and I would reenact touchdown passes, like Tom Brady throwing to Randy Moss. The love I had for the game brought me energy, passion, and comfort.

I always had the dream of playing in the NFL, even at a very young age. I didn't know how I was going to get there, but I knew that it was my dream. And I had a vision; I had lots of visions about it.

When I was about ten years old, it was my dad's birthday, and we went bowling. I beat everyone, and I absolutely loved it and had so much fun. I said, "Hey, this is kind of cool. Let's keep doing this." So, we did. We went every Tuesday night for a long time. Then we started going on Tuesdays and Fridays. This soon became Tuesday, Friday, and Sunday.

Eventually, I said, "Well, why don't I join a league?" So, I did, and I got my own ball and shoes. It got to the point where I was going every single day. I still had a love for football, but it shifted a little bit toward bowling. I competed all over California and Las Vegas and was one of the top-ranked bowlers in the state.

However, I knew I wanted to play quarterback. That was my dream. That was my passion. I didn't know how, but I knew I was going to do it. So, I told my dad, "I want to play football."

Now, keep in mind that my dad knew nothing about American football. He was a professional soccer player in Mexico and even had the opportunity to compete in the U20 World Cup one year. He knew everything about soccer—or, in his terms, "fútbol"—but nothing about American football. So, when I told him I wanted to play football, he was like, "What do you mean?"—I had to explain to him what the game was.

At the time, there was a NYS (National Youth Sports) club, and I asked my dad to take me. He did, but we didn't know anything about how it worked. This was our introduction to the club. When we got there, we discovered that they already had eight teams. Every team selected certain players because some kids had been playing since they were younger. Those guys already kind of knew each other. I was starting at age nine or ten, but many of these guys started when they were five or six. So, I was kind of an outcast; nobody knew me.

There were a lot of kids, but I never got picked. When they told my dad that all the teams were filled, he said, "Why don't you guys just make another team?" because there were a lot of kids who didn't get picked. His point was that it was about learning the game and just having fun at this age. I remember my dad having a long conversation with one of the guys, "We drove 45 minutes to get here. How can we leave kids out?"

Finally, my dad convinced the guy who was in charge to create a ninth team of all the kids who didn't get picked. However, there were only eight coaches. There was no coach

2005 NYS Pitbulls

for the new team. We all looked at each other, asking, "Who's going to be the coach?" None of the other dads raised their hands, so my dad raised his thinking, *Screw it. I'll be the coach. I know nothing, but I'll figure it out.*

My dad was my first official football coach, which a lot of people don't know. He tried hard to learn the game because he knew my passion for it. He wanted to learn it so badly.

I remember our first practice like it was yesterday. My dad owned a party rental business with bounce houses, tables, chairs, and all that. We were practicing at an elementary school, so I said, "We're going to take five bounce houses to practice and use them as tackle dummies." Keep in mind that each one probably weighed four hundred pounds.

My dad loaded up the truck with those five bounce houses, and on the first day, we hit those things for hours. He knew nothing about drills or anything like that. He just knew that you had to know how to tackle. We just did laps, tackled dummies, and threw the ball around for about two hours. I threw up that first practice and thought, *Oh, my gosh. What have I gotten myself into?*

In that group, the divisions weren't based on age but on weight. I was always a big kid, so even though I was only nine or ten years old, I played with 11- and 12-year-olds. Physically, I wasn't as developed as the other guys, but my dad knew I wanted to play quarterback, so he put me in that position—even though I was probably the worst player on the team.

In practice, I got absolutely annihilated by all these bigger guys.

Other parents would say, "Why is your son playing quarterback? What's going on?" Even I was thinking, *Is this really the position I want to play? Everyone wanted to take my head off every play.*

Finally, we got into the season and started playing games. Keep in mind that we were all players that nobody wanted. In the first game, we didn't get a first down, and we lost 50–0. The parents complained to my dad, "What's going on? We have to make a move at quarterback." My dad did not care. He let me in there again and again.

In the second game, we finally got a first down and were so fired up about it. Still, we ended up losing 30–0. A few games later, my dad finally couldn't take the heat anymore. I was beat up and said to him, "Dad, maybe you should let someone else play." So, we brought someone else in as quarterback, but we just kept losing.

Finally, my dad said, "I'm tired of losing, and I want you to play quarterback." Then, he went to different schools and recruited guys to join our team. One day, he brought three guys. These guys were big, maybe 12 or 13 years old. It was the last game of the year, and we happened to be playing the best team in the league.

I threw a couple of passes to the new guys, who broke multiple tackles and scored. We went from not getting a first down to maybe getting one or two a game to beating the best team in the last game of the year. We ended up 1–7 that year. It was a party, though. These guys came in and saved the day. I was the hero, even though I wasn't, because I was just throwing quick passes to them, and they were breaking the tackles. That was my first introduction to football.

Once that season was over, I still loved football, but after getting hit so much and not winning, I didn't really know if it was what I wanted to do. My dad always told me, "These guys are older than you. Just hang in there. It's going to be a lot easier when you start playing with kids your own age because you're a bigger guy." I trusted my dad; whatever he said, I believed it. So, I thought, *Okay, this is fine. I don't like the hits, but I do think that my dad has a point.*

It was around this time that I made the transition to bowling. It was one of those things where I just kind of fell in love with it. Eventually, I was bowling five days a week. I ended up joining the league and got my own shoes and multiple balls. It became a lifestyle at that point.

More time passed, and it was time for me to start middle school —that's where I met my wife. On the first day of middle school, in gym class, the teacher said, "Since it's the first day of school, I want everybody to line up from youngest to oldest."

So, everybody started scrambling around, asking, "When's your birthday?" and then lining up in order. I saw one girl (my future wife) and asked her, "Hey, when's your birthday?"

"August 26," she replied.

"That's my birthday," I told her. It turned out that we were born on the same day of the same year. So, that's how we first met. That was huge for me. Our friendship before we got together was something I'll always cherish. She had a good head on her shoulders, knew what she wanted, and being from a sports background too, we just clicked. We always got along so naturally.

I remember when she would be out there cheering me on, showing up to my practices, and supporting me in everything I did— even before we were more than just best friends. She was always in my corner, and that meant everything. I'd go to practice and then, afterward, walk her all the way home and then go home myself. It was really cool because I had someone at school to share these moments with.

In football games, I went all out. I'd get all my guys together and say, "We've got to do this. We've got to do that." And we got really good. It was a pretty awesome moment because, at the age of 12, I started seeing the results of putting in extra work, whether it was, "Hey guys, let's go lift in the morning before school," or "Let's throw some routes during PE while everybody else is playing and hanging out with their friends." It galvanized us and got us on the same page. Middle school football was like backyard football—we really didn't have plays—we just practiced catching and throwing the ball. We ended up going undefeated and winning the championship.

Fast forward to high school. I thought, *You know what? Let me try this football thing again.* So, I tried out my freshman year, and they basically told me, "We already have our quarterback. You're a big, tall guy, and we could use a tight end in our offense. Why don't you do that instead?"

"Sure," I said. "I'll try it out."

So, I did that, but at the same time, I was bowling. I would get out of football practice and rush to my bowling league. I'd be really tired, so I wasn't bowling as well. That cycle kept repeating.

In high school, we used a wing-T offense. The tight ends were just blocking; they didn't get the ball. That wasn't fun to me. I had a quarterback dream; I didn't have a tight-end dream. That was also the peak of my bowling, so I ended up just saying, "Screw it. I'm not going to play football anymore. I'm going to bowl full time."

I started bowling full-time and did really well, competing in amateur tournaments and traveling to Las Vegas and all over California. I bowled my first 300 game at just 13 years old. For the next three years, I was so locked in on bowling that I hardly went to any football games.

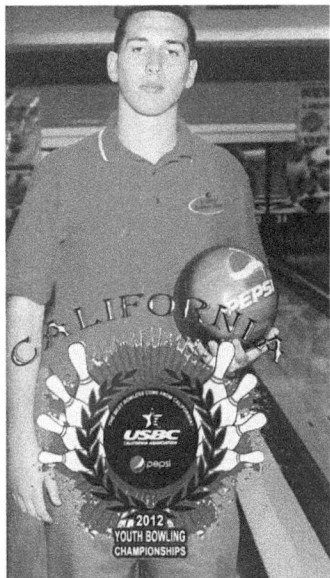

Youth Bowling Pepsi Championship

However, in my senior year, my buddies on the football team convinced me to go to the last home game of the year. I remember this moment like it was yesterday. As I was sitting in the stands, the moment my buddies ran out of a tunnel and onto the field, I got chills. I said, "What am I doing up here? I need to be down there." It just resparked that love I had for playing quarterback as a kid.

Immediately after that game, I said, "Oh, no, I need to try to join the team." They had two games left. The first thing the next morning, I got to school early, went to the coach, and said, "Coach, I know it sounds crazy, but please let me join the team for the last two games of the season."

"I'm sorry, son," he replied. "That's not how we operate. We can't do that."

I was completely devastated. I thought, *What am I going to do?*

7

My dream is to play in the NFL as a quarterback. But my dream is not aligning with what I'm doing. I have to act fast. I have to do something.

My first instinct was that I needed to learn the position. The only thing I knew how to do was throw a nice spiral, and I knew a few routes. I knew nothing about concepts, fronts, or how to read coverage—none of that, I knew nothing. So, I got on YouTube and watched hundreds of videos.

When I told my parents that I was going to pursue football instead of bowling, I remember them saying, "Are you crazy? Like, what is going on? You're doing so well. At this point, you're ranked nationally, and you're about to become a professional bowler." You have to have a certain average to get your PBA card, and I had just hit it.

I told them, "I can bowl when I'm 50 and 60 years old. I really want to pursue this dream of being an NFL quarterback."

As the weeks went on, they were really supportive of everything that was going on. They saw the work ethic. They would walk into my room late and find me still watching YouTube, putting tape in my room, and doing all that.

I would watch hours and hours of videos, like Aaron Rodgers, Drew Brees, and Tom Brady highlights. I'd also watch instructional videos on how to read coverage, how to read fronts, what kind of drops to take with which routes, and all those different things.

I knew I was doing the right thing at that time. I just knew that this was where I was supposed to be. I really enjoyed that whole process of self-learning, and I told myself, *I'm going all in. I can't go in one foot in, one foot out. I'm putting all my eggs in this basket. I want to be an NFL quarterback, and I don't care what anybody tells me—I'm going to do it.*

I reached out to a buddy of mine, David Mundy, because I knew I couldn't do it all on my own. I had to get actual coaching. David's uncle is Akili Smith, who was the third pick in the 1999 NFL draft. He was drafted by the Bengals, and he played quarterback. I said, "Hey,

David, can you please reach out to your uncle and see if he'll train me?"

Finally, I got in touch with Akili, and he said, "Come on, kid. Let's hit the field." He embraced me with open arms and trained me like no other. I mean, he was going four or five times a week. I learned so much in the first month with him. I thought, *Wow! This guy is just amazing. A lot of people have one quarterback coach, but I have to be better than them, so I'm going to go get another one.*

I found another coach, Cree Morris, who was also phenomenal. He was about an hour from me, so I would drive out to train with him once or twice a week. After a session with Cree, I would go to Akili's.

I just knew that I wanted to be different. I did not want to do what everybody else was doing because then I'd be like everybody else. I didn't want to be like everybody else. I wanted to be my own person, but I also wanted to be the best version of myself that I possibly could be.

I trained like this for about five or six months. One day, I threw a ball behind Akili, and he said, "It's fine. You're having a great day. Just put it behind you and move on."

I had an "aha" moment and said to myself, *This is just like when I have three or four strikes in a row and then throw a bad shot and ruin my streak. I know this feeling, and I know how to overcome it.* After I realized this, a lot of things started overlapping between the two sports. I always wanted to be the first one in the bowling alley to get there and bowl, and now I wanted to be the first one on the field.

Another thing Akili started talking about was how to spin the ball. Finally, it clicked for me. I started throwing the ball, and it was coming out with more velocity and more spin. I realized that it was just like bowling, but overhand. It was the same exact motion. So, when he told me that, it was another aha moment: "I'm good at bowling, so I can be good at this, too. I've already trained a lot of these different muscles that I'm using for football."

This was my passion as a kid. I wanted to be an NFL quarterback, and I've always had it ingrained in me to be different. You can't do what everybody else is doing because then you're going to be like everybody else. If you want to be the best, you have to do what the best do.

I remember watching videos of Kobe Bryant and him saying, "Get up at 3:00 a.m., go to the gym at four, and work out from four to six. Then go get a snack. From eight to nine, go to the basketball court and shoot some hoops. Then go home and eat, recover, and maybe take a nap. Afterward, go back to the gym and run for two hours. Then have dinner. After that, go back to the gym again."

That's four or five workouts in one day. When you do that over and over and over again throughout your life, you're going to be light years ahead of everybody else. Those were some of the types of videos I would always watch—on motivation, passion, and how to be the best. I was also lucky to have a very good support system. My parents were professionals, and they've guided me.

In high school, the moment that the coach told me, "We're going to move you to tight end," I knew right away that that wasn't what I wanted to do. At the time, I did what was best for the team because I wanted to be a team guy, but deep in my heart, I knew that that was not what my passion was or what I wanted to do. So, I battled between following what the coach said and what I wanted to do. Luckily, I had bowling as an easy out. I was easily able to say, "Well, you know what? I'm just not going to do this football thing anymore because it's not what I want to do."

People know what they want. You might not think that you can get there, but you know what you want to do. You can't settle for anything else. If you want something, you've got to get out of your comfort zone and make it happen. I knew my passion at a young age —I just knew it.

I'd carry the football around, throw it in the store in the aisles, and go to sleep with it. I told myself, *I don't care what anybody says to me. I know what I want. And this is what I want.*

That is what it takes. You have to use every single resource possible to get it done. Whether it's YouTube, getting coaching, or whatever, if you want something bad enough, you will get it done.

You have to be able to overcome the little voice in the back of your mind that tells you, "Am I crazy?" I had that voice. I mean, I was about to become a professional bowler at 16 years old. I just knew in my heart that it wasn't the right time. I knew it. I knew my passion was playing quarterback.

Again, it's a calculated risk, right? I'm not five foot trying to play in the NBA. I fit the mold. I'm six foot three, 215, 220 pounds, your typical size for a quarterback. I can also throw the ball well. So, my mold fits my dream. It's not just a wacky risk or some random thing.

The point is, when you want something, you have to go for it.

A lot of people think that they want something bad enough, but do they really? I didn't care about anything else. I dreamed about football. I thought about football all day. I drew plays in the classroom. I had an obsession with this game. If you have that obsession, take a leap of faith and go for it.

AKILI SMITH – FORMER NFL QB AND LUIS' MENTOR

I was the first person who really started to teach Luis the foundation of quarterback play. When he was at Otay, they decided to go a different route with a different quarterback. Luis was playing tight end, but he was clearly the better quarterback.

After that took place, he said, "Forget it. I want to be a full-fledged quarterback." And then that's when we started to work on the one-step drop from the gun, the three-step drop from the gun, and the three-step drop from under center, understanding route concepts and route depth and making sure your shoulders are level, and you're able to rotate and use the torque that you need to be an accurate quarterback.

And he picked it up quite quickly.

I don't believe I've ever had a quarterback who works as hard as Luis; his determination to be successful is just unmatched. There have been times when I'm going out there, and I just completely let him take the workout because he's that accurate with his information. He understands the concepts.

He understands route depth. He understands protections and stuff like that to where I will literally just go out there and just record and show him if his front shoulder was up just a little bit, or if his front knee wasn't perfectly slightly bent, or if we need to try to put some air under a ball or anything like that. I would show him that, but outside of that, I mean, man, Luis is a perfectionist, and it shows.

Luis is the type of guy you introduce your daughter to. Let me just say that. That's it in a nutshell.

If you were looking for an athlete who played football and you wanted him to be like the other athletes who are womanizers and different things like that, then Luis is not your guy. But if you want a guy who's going to come home every night, raise his kids, do things the right way, and be respectful and upright in the community, then Luis Perez fits that bill.

It's funny because they say that about my son. Luis's parents and the village that he's a part of raised him properly. And that's what it's about. You have to surround yourself with good people, and that village has to be united in its goal—to help someone like Luis Perez get to where he needs to be. And that's as a professional quarterback.

And then, obviously, my son, Akili Smith Jr., who's a quarterback at Oregon—Luis actually worked with him as well. And he's one of the only quarterback coaches that Akili Smith Jr. has worked with. So, I brought Luis to the table for my son because I know what type of morals and ethics Luis practices.

TWO
JUNIOR COLLEGE CHALLENGES AND TRIUMPHS

I asked Akili Smith, "What do I do next? I want to get to the NFL. This is my end goal. Help me build my path to get there."

He had a relationship with Ed Carberry, the head coach at South-western College. When he told me that, I got so excited. Even though I didn't play football in high school, I still might have an opportunity to play in junior college. He made the call and said, "All right, go to his office and talk to him."

I went to see Ed and told him, "Hey, coach. My name is Luis Perez. I want to be your next quarterback."

He kind of chuckled a little bit and replied, "Okay. Where did you play high school football?"

"Well, coach," I said, "actually, I didn't play high school football."

"Huh? What do you mean?"

"Yeah, I was a bowler."

"Well, all right, son," he said. "We have practice at this time. I can't tell you no because we're a junior college. Anybody can go to the tryout. So, here are the times, and here are the dates."

I showed up to practice on the first day, and there were nine quarterbacks. I was ninth out of the nine by default because I was the only one who did not play high school football. When we got our equipment—since I was the last one—they didn't have a helmet my size, so they gave me an extra-large helmet with a lineman facemask.

At the time, I thought, *Oh, this is cool.* I didn't really know much. But the other guys made fun of me: "Why do you have a lineman helmet on?" I was the only guy who had one, and it was heavy. In practice, I couldn't even see because the facemask blocked my vision. I thought, *Screw this. I need to get my own helmet because this is not going to cut it.*

I worked on the weekends for my dad's party business to save up some money to get myself a helmet, and it was a lot better. I just showed up every day. The only quarterbacks who got reps were the top four guys. All the other guys got no reps. But little by little, people started dropping, switching positions, or finding their way to different sports.

Eventually, the coach told me, "Luis, we have a lot of quarterbacks right now. You're not getting any reps, so we're going to have to cut you."

"I'm sorry, coach," I said. "With all due respect, I'm not going anywhere because I haven't gotten an opportunity to show you what I can do."

"Fine," he replied. "You can keep coming, but you're not getting any reps."

That happened twice: in the spring of 2013 and at the beginning of summer. But I just kept showing up. My persistence never stopped. I knew this was what I wanted. I knew I could do it because I knew that when I set my mind to something, I could get it done. The passion was just too much.

I was at the bottom, but I just kept showing up—first one there, last one to leave. That was ingrained in me.

Finally, people started noticing: "Hey, who is this guy?" And again, guys were dropping out, switching positions, transferring schools, getting hurt, whatever the case might be. Eventually, in the summer of 2013, there were only four of us, and I finally started getting some reps. Everybody was looking at me sideways like, "This guy might have something to him."

We had a set starter who was a sophomore. He had started the year before, and his name was Frank Foster. He was a stud, an absolute stud. This guy was amazing in the weight room and just a smart, cool guy. I really enjoyed my time with him.

Little by little, I just kept showing up and kept competing. Then we had a scrimmage, and I did really well. I was so nervous because I didn't know what string I was going to be. I just knew they had their starter, and the second, third, and fourth strings were all battling for the backup spot.

The coach brought me into his office and said, "Luis, I'm really proud of you. You've done everything right. You showed up, and you were persistent. I want you to be the backup quarterback."

This took a huge weight off my back. I thought, *Okay. People are noticing me. I can do this.* That gave me more confidence. Then I wondered, *Should I tell my parents that I'm getting ready to do this?* They knew that I was pursuing becoming a quarterback, but they didn't really know the details. Ultimately, I decided not to tell them yet.

I ended camp strong, and in week three of the season, Frank Foster separated his AC joint. Everyone was looking at me, like, "You're in, Luis."

I went out there, and the coach called the play. All I could think was, *Whoa, I'm on the field!* I actually got a delay-of-game penalty on my first play. The coaches yelled, "Luis, snap the ball. What's wrong?" So, I pulled myself together.

We were down two touchdowns, and I remember just getting in the zone, thinking, *This is what I worked for. This is my opportunity.* A lot of people go through life not receiving an opportunity like this, and I could not let this one pass me by.

I was so in the zone that it was like nothing else mattered. I was completely locked in and didn't hear the crowd. It was just about executing to the best of my ability—every single play. I ended up throwing two touchdown passes in the fourth quarter, and we came back to win the game. I went to the coach and said, "I told you I could do it." And he just laughed. The power of persistence is such a big thing: being able to set your mind on something and not take no for an answer because you know what you are capable of and what you want.

After that game, I kept thinking, *Wow, I really did this. I really did this.* Despite my exhilaration, I didn't know if I would start the next game.

The next day, the coaches told me Frank's diagnosis and said, "He's probably going to be out for a couple of weeks, so you're going to be the quarterback moving forward." I was fired up, and once they gave me the green light, I went through a couple of practices. Sure enough, I was getting all the reps, and I was thrilled.

Two days before the next game, I was having dinner with my family, and I told them, "Hey, guys, I'm starting at quarterback for Southwestern. I got a game on Saturday at Olympian High School. Do you guys want to come?"

They stared at me and said, "What? What do you mean? You're starting?"

"Yeah," I said. "I'm starting." They were in complete shock, so I told them what had happened.

"Wow," they said. "All your hard work's paying off."

My grandma, who was battling cancer, made a huge effort to go to the game. She was walking around with an oxygen tank, but she was so supportive. She was like my second mom. I mean, my grandparents lived next door to us—literally, we were neighbors. So, I would always go over and tell her how my practices were going. I felt really comfortable talking about that with her and my grandpa.

In the next game, it was such a surreal feeling to go out there and perform the way that I did, with four touchdowns and over three hundred yards. To top it all off, we were playing an undefeated team, but we went out there and just dominated.

Everyone was looking at me like, "Who is this guy? Where did this guy even come from?" Even my head coach was like, "Whoa, you're playing phenomenally. Great job." I just remember tearing up after the game. After all the hard work, I was finally able to show everyone what I could do. I was on the right track. I knew that this was the path I needed to be on.

The next week, we played another good team, and we had a very good game plan. I was excited to go out there and play. My whole family was there.

I went out there, and we were dominating, 21–0 in the first quarter. I was fired up. *Oh, yeah,* I thought. *This is going to be my year. I'm going to get a scholarship.* Soon, we were up 28–0, and I remember going out there for another drive and calling a read option.

Southwestern College, Chula Vista, California (2013–2014)

I pulled the ball and started running, and a linebacker grabbed me, pinned me down, and spun me. As I was spinning, a lineman fell on the back of my leg, and I remember thinking, *Oh, man, this doesn't feel good.* My leg felt really hot and numb.

I stayed in for a couple more plays, and when the drive ended, I returned to the sideline. The doctor checked me out and said, "We've got to get an X-ray to make sure it's not broken."

Sure enough, when the X-ray came back, the doctor said, "Son, you fractured your fibula. You're going to be out for the year."

I just remember sitting back and asking God, "Why do you put all these things in front of me, the success, all that, to just take it away in the blink of an eye?"

I got surgery on Halloween in 2013, and I cried every day because I thought that I had reached my goal and was on the right track. Then things did a complete 180. I got to the top of the mountain, and I broke my leg and went right back down. The emotions were just insane. Luckily, again, I had a good support system with my girlfriend at the time, my wife now, and my parents and brothers.

I remember thinking, *Is this a sign from God telling me that football is not for me? Like, Yes, you did great. It was fun. You did an amazing job, but this is not your calling. You need to bowl.*

I had that constant battle throughout rehab. Finally, I got all through that and was able to come back and practice. I thought, *No, this is right. The injury was just a small hurdle. What doesn't kill you makes you stronger. This is supposed to be part of my journey.*

When I was finally ready to go, the coach brought me in to tell me, "We just got a new quarterback. He's a Division I bounce-back who was the Southern California player of the year in high school here in San Diego."

I was devastated. I had done all that rehab, everything to be the starting quarterback again this year, and they just brought a D-I bounce-back and handed him the keys. I remember thinking, *I've got to do more.* Obviously, I hadn't done well enough for them to say, "This is your job."

So, I just kept showing up. I knew that I was playing catch-up.

This guy had played for four years in high school, while I hadn't. "I have to do more. Everybody's ahead of me. They did four years in high school." I constantly played that in my head, over and over and over.

I went to camp, and he was already taking most of the reps. We were battling it out, but I was still not 100% healthy. I was not playing to the best of my ability. I remember the coach brought me in and said, "We're going to go with the other quarterback." Once again, I was devastated. My emotions were up and down like a rollercoaster.

In week three of the season, we're down two touchdowns in the fourth quarter. He gets hurt—bruised ribs. He comes out of the game. Here we go all over again. I come in, get in the zone, throw two touchdown passes, and bring us back.

We won the game. This time, instead of just thinking *I told you so,* I was screaming it in the coach's face.

"Don't you ever not start me again!" I completely let him have it. "What are you doing? What were you thinking?"

I quickly realized that wasn't the right thing to do. My emotions overflowed, and I let them spill.

I was the starting quarterback, but they still wanted to implement the other guy into the offense. So, we just kept going back and forth, sharing reps, sharing reps, sharing reps. I knew I had to be the first one there. I had to outdo him in every single thing I did. Finally, they just said, "All right, you're the guy, Luis."

In the last few games of the season, we did really well and ended up going to the championship game, which was a bittersweet moment for me.

As I mentioned, my grandma was battling cancer all year, but she went to as many games as she could. She would be exhausted going up the stands, and I remember thinking, *Wow, my grandma's really coming out here to my games. She truly believes in me.*

Toward the end, she couldn't attend many because her condition had become too critical, eventually leading to her being admitted to the hospital.

I always looked for my family in the stands, and during the championship game, I spotted them there. I knew my grandma was in the hospital, but I thought she was stable and everything was okay.

At halftime, after returning from the locker room, when I looked up in the stands, my family wasn't there anymore. *That's weird,* I thought. *I hope everything's all right.*

We won the championship. We were all ecstatic, celebrating—even had a little ceremony. Everything was great, but something felt off. My family wasn't there on the field with all the other families.

I rushed to my phone and saw a flood of missed calls and text messages: *"You need to come to the hospital right now. Your grandma's not doing well. She only has a few moments left."*

I didn't even change. I just took off my pads and said, "Bye, guys. I love you all, but I've got to go." Then I left.

When I got to the hospital, my grandma was intubated, and everyone was distraught. My emotions were in turmoil. It had been such a good day. We'd just won the championship. I'd just achieved a major goal of mine. But at the same time, my grandma, my second mom, was on the verge of losing her life.

I went in to see her and said, "Grandma, we won the championship." She couldn't communicate with me, so I told her, "If you can hear me, squeeze my hand," and she did. She knew—something she had wanted so badly for me.

A few hours later, my grandma passed. I will always feel grateful for being able to make it by her side.

About a week before that, she talked to me about the importance of continuing to push for my dream, how proud she was of me for pursuing playing quarterback, and how she never wanted that to go away.

The moment she passed, I knew my motivation was only that much stronger.

She loved my wife. At the time, nobody knew I was about to propose—except for my grandma. I'm so glad I told her. Her support meant the world to me; she truly wanted this dream for me.

That year I ended up throwing 18 touchdowns with only three interceptions. We went 10–1. It was one of the hardest years of my life yet there were some moments of light.

A couple of weeks passed as we grieved. Then, in January 2015, my wife and I got married in a small ceremony in my mother-in-law's backyard.

After the wedding, I started wondering, *What's next?* I knew I was going to play football somewhere and that I wanted to get a scholarship. I also knew that with the

Wedding Day

awards I had earned there was a possibility I would get some form of scholarship. My dream was to play Division I football, so I emailed every single D-I school in the country. Every single one. I sent out a bio of my accolades, film, and my stats.

The responses were all along the lines of, "Love your film, but you only played one year." Some wouldn't even bother getting back to me.

Someone said, "You want a preferred walk-on spot? We have one for you."

I replied, "No, I want a scholarship. I don't want my parents to have the burden of paying for my school. I want to have my school paid for."

After a while, everything went blank, and I had nothing. I mean, I had absolutely nothing. A lot of small schools offered me scholarships, but no Division I schools. Months went by, and I thought, *What am I going to do?*

Finally, UC Davis called me and told me that they were interested. "We want to bring you on a visit and talk some ball with you."

So my wife and I drove to UC Davis, about a ten-hour drive from where we lived. We met with the coach, Kevin Daft. When I was looking up this coaching staff, I discovered that Kevin was Aaron Rodgers's coach when he was at Cal. So, I was thinking, *Wow! This is amazing. I get to be coached by the same guy Aaron Rodgers got coached by.*

We talked ball for a while, and Kevin and the other coaches were intrigued by my IQ. They were also intrigued by the fact that I was a one-year starter and didn't play in high school, and they loved my size. Finally, they said, "We're going to offer you a scholarship."

I was thrilled. I told my parents, and they threw a little surprise party for me when we arrived. We were all so excited because we didn't know how the process worked. We just thought, if somebody offers you a scholarship, that's it. You're in.

After the party, I had a moment with my wife where we said to one another, "Wow, we're really going to do this together." My wife wanted to be an animal science major, and they had one of the top animal science programs in the country, so it was a win for both of us.

But then bad news hit. After training for about a week or two, I got a call from the head coach. He said, "Luis, we have some bad news for you. Your math is not transferable to a UC school, only to a California State school, so we're not going to be able to offer you a scholarship."

"You have to be kidding me." This was everything we wanted. Everything had aligned perfectly. Again, we were back to square one, with nowhere to play ball and no Division I scholarships. I didn't know what to do.

A few more weeks passed, and I thought, *I have to make a move. I can't just be stagnant. I have to figure out what to do.* I kept emailing schools, but I wasn't hearing from any Division I schools. It was now June 2015, and people were getting ready to report for the summer. So, I said, "If Division I is not going to do it, it's going to be Division II."

I researched which Division II quarterbacks had made it to the NFL and came across a guy named Dustin Vaughan, who was with the Cowboys. Digging deeper, I found out he had played at West Texas A&M under Coach Colby Carthel.

I did some more research and discovered that Coach Carthel was now at Texas A&M Commerce, now known as East Texas A&M. I said to myself, *If this guy could do it, I can do it, too.* " I reached out to him through Twitter (now known now as X), and said, *"These are my stats. This is what I do. I'd love to come play for you guys."*

They ended up flying out to San Diego and went to Southwestern College to watch me throw. After about 15 throws, they said, "Hey, we want to offer you a scholarship."

I was ecstatic. I'd done all this research and finally gotten the scholarship. It was not necessarily what I wanted, nor my first choice, but at least I was on the right path. The moment I accepted that scholarship to go to Texas A&M Commerce, I felt relieved. I knew I was headed in the right direction. *My goal was now within reach.*

In life, the things you want don't just get handed to you. You have to earn them. One of the positives of this is that the situations and obstacles that you go through make the moment. Everything that I had gone through, breaking my leg, not playing in high school, switching positions, sharing time, and waiting for somebody to get hurt again, made getting this scholarship so much more special than it would have been if I'd just gone the traditional route.

My closing thought is *don't give up.* Just put one foot in front of the other. You're going to fall, but it's how you get up and then continue to get up.

Once I signed the papers to go to East Texas A&M, my wife and I looked at each other and said, "All right, let's do this." We packed up the U-Haul and drove to Texas.

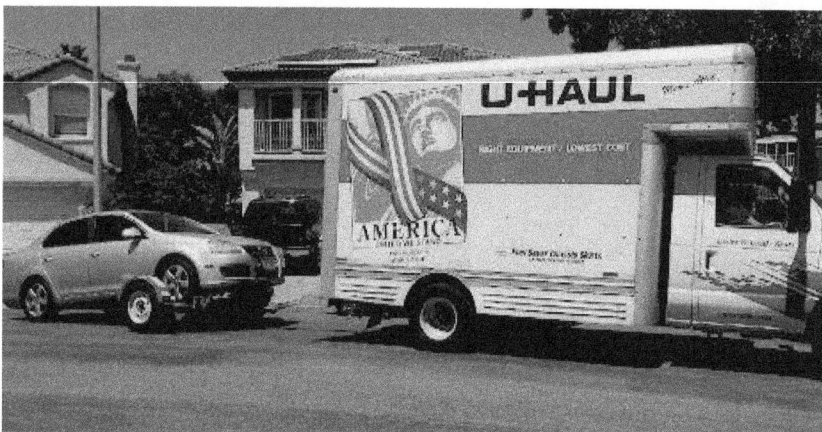

Packed up and headed to Texas

ED CARBERRY – FORMER SOUTHWESTERN COLLEGE HEAD COACH

I was his coach back in 2013 and 2014. I was the head coach, and Luis and I worked directly together.

He was our quarterback. When it comes to leadership, he's top-notch. I've been a coach for 46 years, and he's up there with any of them in terms of his ability to lead and get people going in the right direction. He's as hard a working guy as there is.

I saw his dedication firsthand both at Southwestern and while he was in the NFL. I would watch him over and over again from my office window when he would come out in the offseason to train in the early mornings at Southwestern.

There's a difference between guys who like to play quarterback and guys who are quarterbacks. And his effort and all the things that go around with it are second to none. After practice, while most guys were heading home, Luis would stay out on the field with four or five teammates, running routes to perfect his timing and throwing mechanics.

We spent a lot of time watching film together, just talking about football. It was always a great experience. We had a great time and enjoyed every minute of it.

And he had to battle. He battled injuries. He broke his leg against Compton Community College. The very next practice after surgery, he showed up in full pads with a cast. I even took a picture; I was in such disbelief. Then, we had our school banquet, and my mom was there. She was fired up about it. He ended up sitting for three hours at the banquet with a cast on his leg. That says a lot about him. Everybody wants that kind of guy.

He and I talk quite a bit during the offseason. Sometimes, he may have a question, or I have a question with him, and we get a chance to take care of football that way. Then we just have a fun time, talking about how things are going.

I was joking with him yesterday while we were setting up this interview. I told everyone on the other end that they were dealing with the guy who tried to cut him. He laughed and said, "With the way I played back then, I would've cut me, too."

We had nine quarterbacks, two of whom were Division I scholarship players. In fact, two others had already earned Division I scholarships. There were two key moments I remember. First, in our season opener, Luis hadn't played much because the guy ahead of him, who was the Division I scholarship player and the Athlete of the Year in San Diego, was starting. At halftime, Luis came up to me and said, "Coach, what's going on? I need to get in the game. I need some film, and I could do better."

We were going back and forth, figuring things out. At halftime, Luis came into the locker room while I was preparing to talk to the players. The other quarterback, who was leading the charge, was having fun with a boombox on his shoulder. But when I went to check on Luis, I found him in a different part of the locker room. He had gathered all the offensive players and was coaching them up. He had paper and pencil in hand, *already explaining the next play. I just turned around and walked away—he had everything under control.*

Then, the starting quarterback ahead of Luis got injured, which gave Luis the opportunity to step up even more. What followed was the emergence of an exceptional player on the field. On weekends, after the games, his family would catch passes with him as part of his training. It was a sight to see. Luis was that kind of player—fully committed, driven, and always putting in the work.

His story is so unique. I think that his book is going to inspire a lot of people in that it shows that there's no one path to success.

He came in and had never played football. He came up to me as a freshman in college. We tried to move him to a different position. He came up about midway through the summer.

He came up to me and said, "What am I going to do?"

I said, "Well, you can change positions." I gave him about four or five options.

I tried to switch his position. I told him he wasn't going to get any reps, but he just kept showing up. He was the first one there and the last one to leave. Little by little, he gained my trust, and ultimately, I gave him the opportunity for the backup role. All it took for us to witness the impossible was that we started to get hurt.

I even told him I would call Grossmont College and Mesa College and ask them to see if I could get him over there because never in a million years did I think he was going to be my starting quarterback. Eventually, I gave him a chance as the backup quarterback due to injuries, and he exceeded all expectations. I never imagined he would become the starting quarterback; I even considered calling colleges on his behalf.

It was a blessing for us. He threw the ball like no one else. He's exceptionally skilled as a full-time player. He has an incredible ability to read the defense—there's nothing a defense can throw at him that he can't overcome. His response to any challenge from the defense was always simple: "They can't be everywhere."

THREE
NEW BEGINNINGS IN TEXAS

W e packed our bags and headed to Commerce, Texas, in a big U-Haul loaded with all our stuff and towing my 2008 Volkswagen Jetta. The trip took 23 hours, and it was definitely an experience. I had never done a road trip that long, but it was fun. We were on our way to embark on this next journey together. Luckily, my parents were able to help out, so they came along.

When we got to Commerce, the first thing that hit us in the face was the heat in the middle of July. Being from San Diego, this was *not* something I was used to. There was some adjusting to be done.

I think there were only about four or five thousand people living in the town, not including the students. We ended up loving the small-town feel, where everyone knew each other. Even shops would shut down on game days. I was excited about the new opportunities and knew this was going to be memorable.

I was moving across the country, but my goal was always in mind. I knew that I wanted to go to the NFL and that this was the route I had to take, so I was all in.

A few weeks later, once we were settled in, I attended my first workout. I went out there with a water bottle, but everyone else had ice coolers. I thought, *Oh, that's odd.* That first day, we ran for about an hour and a half, did some speed stuff, hit the weight room, and did some conditioning.

By then, my water was completely hot, and my cleats were melting on the bottom. I quickly realized why people brought those ice coolers. It was probably one of the toughest workouts I've had in my life, I wasn't used to the heat.

I was throwing up and on the verge of passing out. But I embraced it because I knew this was a big step for me and good was going to come from it. I had that no pain, no gain mentality. I was getting better. If it were easy and I wasn't throwing up and exhausted, I wouldn't be getting better. So, I needed to take this step and dive in and say, "You know what? This is part of it, and I'm only going to get better from here."

At the start of that year's season, they brought me into the office and told me, "We already have our starter. You're coming in so late. You are going to redshift this year."

At the time, I didn't really know what that meant. They explained, "This doesn't count as a year of eligibility, so you can develop as a player, get bigger, faster, stronger, learn the game more. And next year, you can compete for the starting job."

Great, I thought. *Another year of school paid for and another year of development.* I felt like I was so far behind due to not playing high school football. I needed more experience to really perform the way that I needed to in order to make it to the NFL. So, I believed that being redshirted was a great thing.

For a whole year, I lifted with the freshmen at five in the morning and was basically a board holder during games. I wasn't playing, but I would go and jot down every single play. Then I would tell the quarterbacks and coach what I was seeing during the games, trying to help with any input I had.

For the whole year, I just sat back and observed everything that went on: how college football operated, what the coach wanted from the quarterback, how he wanted the offense to run, and the leadership aspect of it.

Learning a playbook was always tough. I came from a system in junior college that was very simple and easy to learn. This offense was a little more complex. Again, there are different ways to learn, and I'm somebody who has to go out and do it. I can also learn from reading, but back then, I was more of a visual guy and had to do it and see it done over and over again.

I had my wife read me the plays. She also learned the signals and signaled to me throughout the day, asking, "What do you have on this play?" It was awesome having her there to help me in any way she could.

We had a pretty good year and ended up going to the playoffs and losing in the first round. I remember thinking, *This is not what I want to do. I don't want to go to the playoffs and lose in the first round. This is definitely not a good feeling.* So, I embraced that, I took that, and I decided, *You know what? I need to do something about this.*

Again, success is about being different. If you do what everybody else does, you're going to be like everybody else. You have to stand out in whatever you do.

I remember reflecting on why I chose Commerce. I told myself, *Well, Dustin Vaughn made it to the NFL from Division II. I can do it, too.* That was how I approached everything in life. I knew that if I did what I was supposed to do—grow bigger and faster, learn the leadership aspect of being a quarterback, and learn the playbook—I'd get to where I wanted to go.

When the season was over, I had to make a transition. My mindset was now a little bit different. Now I was competing for a spot. This is where everything would get good because now I was ready to step onto the field and perform.

I always had faith. I had faith that I was where I was supposed to be and on my way to where I wanted to go. I had a vision. I'll have to admit, at times, I was homesick. We were now away from family living where there was only a Walmart and a couple of food places within a 40-mile radius. You had to drive 45 minutes to get anywhere else. All that stuff was an adjustment, but we knew there was a bigger picture—big risk, big reward—so we took a leap of faith.

After the first year, I knew that I was in the right spot.

When that year ended (December 2015), we went back to California for the holidays. While there, I did whatever I could to stay in shape.

Now, at that time, there was a quarterback coach named George Whitfield who trained big-time quarterbacks Andrew Luck, Cam Newton, and Johnny Manziel. This guy was very hard to get to. You couldn't just pick up the phone, find the guy's phone number, and call him.

I tried for weeks and weeks to get in touch with him. Finally, I got a hold of his assistant, who told me where and when they were going to have a session. However, when I went to the workout, George was not there, just the assistant. I wanted to meet George, though, not only to learn from him, but I knew that he had good connections. I had to be around the right people to reach my goal. I did the workout with the assistant, and it went well.

About a week later, I found out through a buddy of mine who was at that session that a group of quarterbacks—Brandon Wimbush, Jarrett Guarantano, Josh Allen, Johnny Manziel, and Cam Newton—were having a private workout at Cathedral High School with George. College football analyst Kirk Herbstreit was there as well.

I reached out to the assistant and asked, *"Hey, can I go to this workout?"*

Never got a response.

I ended up going anyway and snuck in. I sat at the top of the bleachers, and I looked down and saw them all there. I thought, *Should I just go down there? What should I do?"*

I ended up calling the assistant to see if I could join them. However, when he picked up his phone, he saw it was me and put it back down.

I thought, *Man, this guy's not going to answer the phone.* But that just fueled my desire: *You know what? What's the worst thing that could happen? I'm going to go down there.*

When I went down, the assistant was completely shocked, "Whoa, what are you doing here?"

Then George said, "Hey, man, you want to hop in?"

"Sure!" I immediately replied.

Initially, all I was doing was snapping the balls to the quarterback. Then George said, "Why don't you get a few throws in and let me see what you can do?" So, I went out there and started spinning the ball, and everyone was looking at me like, *Who is this guy?*

Kirk Herbstreit came up to me and said, "Where do you play? You can spin it really well." I told him my story, and he was intrigued. In the end, I absolutely killed the workout. From then on, George and I have had a good relationship.

I realized my dream of playing in the NFL would take sacrifice, dedication, and hard work. Back in Texas, I remember getting up at 5 a.m., working out until seven o'clock, and then watching film. I embraced the structure and loved it—ultimately, that's all I was there for.

In my eyes, I was there just to play football and do whatever I could to make it to the NFL. That goal never changed. I just knew that all these sacrifices were going to pay off at some point. I didn't know when, and I didn't know how, but I knew, at some point, they would.

So, I stayed the course and just kept showing up. I remember waking up in the mornings thinking, *Do I really want to do this?* Then I would think, *Well, if it were easy, everybody would do it. So, if this is the emotion I'm feeling right now, but I go do it anyway, I'm already ahead of a lot of people.*

That motivated me. If somebody said, "No, man, I don't feel like working out," my response was, "Let's go. We've got to do it." The odds are that if you don't want to do it, neither does everyone else. But the satisfaction that you get from actually going and doing the workout far outweighs that of not working out.

I wanted everybody on the team to believe that way too, because everything's about culture in football. You can have the best players, the best athletes, and the best coaching, but if it's not cohesive and they're not playing as one unit, it's not going to work. It's important to have a support system.

Having big dreams isn't easy. I leaned on my family and my mentors back home who were guiding me through the process. They were all very supportive. You can't do it alone, right? I didn't get to where I am on my own. A lot of people sacrificed their time to help me get to where I am today.

I took a big risk, going all the way to Commerce, Texas, but with big risk comes high reward. I took a leap of faith, and I had the vision. To me, that was the most important thing.

The vision was where I wanted to go. So, I mapped out my quest of how to get there. Once it's mapped out, it's a day-to-day process. Then, one day, you look up, and you're already a year in. I trusted the process and then restarted again every year. I set my goals and just kept achieving them, short-term and long-term.

I knew that if I had faith, a vision, and put my head down and worked hard, it would benefit me and put me on the right path to making my NFL dream come true.

FOUR
BECOMING A LEADER

A ll I could think was, *I have to win that starting job this year. For me to reach my goal, I have to win the starting job.*

My wife would quiz me on our plays. She'd tell me the play, and I'd have to memorize it and then say it back to her.

In my mind I would tell myself, *I'm so far behind. I have to outwork every single person. I haven't played as long as they have, which means I'm already at least four years behind. I have to play catch up, I have to be different and do what people aren't doing.*

Spring ball started. By now, everybody on the team knew that I was competing for the starting job. I told the coach, "I'm ready to be your quarterback, and I'm ready to take this team as far as it's ever been."

He looked at me and said, "I believe in you. I believe in you."

That gave me such a warm feeling because I'd never had that. In junior college, it was always like, "You're not good enough," or "You only played one year." People doubted me, but I want to make this clear: I was never motivated by a desire to prove all those people wrong. I didn't care about that. I knew what I was.

But for all those people who believed in me—my family, my

mentors, close friends—I wanted to prove them right. They knew that I could do it. They knew all the work I put in, and they knew how passionate I was about achieving this dream.

During spring ball, I was splitting reps with another quarterback. He was a good football player, and now a lifelong friend. But back then, we were battling it out. We'd have good days and bad days. We were grinding. We had a spring game, and we both did well. When it was over, I prayed, "Please let me be the starter."

At the end of the school year, I had an exit meeting with my coach. I didn't know if I had done enough. I asked him, "Coach, what do you think? Am I going to be your quarterback? What do you think?"

"Oh, son," he said, "it's way too early. You're going to have to perform in camp. I'm not naming the starter until training camp."

It's hard to believe now, but back then, I didn't know that process. I thought I would win the starting job in spring ball. So after that meeting, I remember thinking, *the job's not finished.*

We drove back to California for summer, my wife quizzed me the whole way there. Once there, I decided that I had to train with the best. I needed to come back better. I heard about a trainer, Todd Durkin.

Todd is a phenomenal human being, a phenomenal coach, and a great mentor of mine to this day. He just brightens the whole room. He's a guy you want to be around at all times, and his smile is infectious. I can't thank him enough.

However, at the time, I had no idea how to get in contact with him. I reached out to different buddies of mine, but nobody really knew him. He's kind of an exclusive guy.

I said, "I'm just going to show up." So, I showed up one day and said to him, "Hey, can you train me?"

"Well," he said, "I'm training Drew Brees, Darren Sproles, Manti Te'o, Brandin Cooks, Chase Daniel, all these guys, but I can send you to my assistant, Charles."

"Okay, that's fine," I replied. So, I had a one-on-one with Charles, who is an amazing guy.

I got bigger, faster, and stronger, and my hope was that one day, Todd Durkin would ask me, "Do you want to come out to the field with the pro guys?" I was just waiting. I didn't know if it was going to happen, but I manifested that. I dreamed about that. I prayed about that. I would think, *Please, just please ask me that.*

Finally, after a few weeks, sure enough, I was finishing my workout with Charles, and the pro guys were coming in. Todd Durkin said to me, "The pro guys are coming out to the field. Do you want to come out?"

"Heck yes," I said. "Absolutely."

The first day when I was out there with Drew Brees, Darren Sproles, Chase Daniel, and all these guys. I thought, *Wow, these are pro guys. This is the standard. This is what I need to look like if I want to be at that level.* That first throwing session, I went out there and just watched.

Drew and Chase were throwing the ball on the money, and all these great receivers were catching the ball so smoothly. I just observed. I don't think I got to throw for the first couple of sessions. I just watched and snapped the ball to them, observing how they communicated.

Those four or five sessions I had of just observing changed my life. It was amazing how Drew communicated with his teammates. He knew how to talk to Darren Sproles. He knew how to talk to Michael Thomas. He knew how to talk to all these guys to get the best out of them. I really took that as a learning experience.

I had taken a leadership course back at Southwestern. At the time, leadership hadn't been as important to me. But when I started hearing Drew talk, I had flashbacks of that course and thought, *This is what they were talking about. This is how I can apply that to my current profession.*

I was also impressed by the way Drew was able to turn on and off his switch. We would be laughing before we started, but the moment Todd Durkin said, "We're ready to rock and roll," there was no talking, and Drew was all business. I just knew that that was the right way. *Hall of Fame quarterback, this is how he does it. This is the blueprint. I want to follow in his footsteps.*

The guy was such an amazing person on top of that. Everybody always talks about when players become famous, how they lose their humbleness and all that—everything goes to their head. But Drew Brees is one of the kindest, humblest guys I've met in my life; he was always willing to help.

It was kind of a dream come true. Keep in mind that I was born and raised in San Diego, and I'd grown up a Chargers fan. Now, I was training with my idol. I mean, I felt like saying, "Somebody pinch me. Is this real right now? Am I really training next to Drew Brees?"

I was able to train with him that entire off-season. Those were memorable times. Throughout that process, he worked with a personal quarterback coach named Tom House. Drew saw that I was consistent and that I was the first one there and the last one to leave. He saw my hunger; he saw my passion. He was the same: before we started the throwing session with all the receivers, he was there about an hour and 30 minutes early with his quarterback coach, training. I would always get there early so I would get a chance to see the tail end of his sessions.

One day, days before I had to return to Texas for the season, he came up to me and said, "Luis, do you want to come out with my quarterback coach and watch?"

"Heck yeah," I said.

The technical savvy, the biomechanical aspect of playing quarterback, the rotational power—I felt like I learned more than I ever had in those four or five sessions with Tom House and Drew Brees. I took that and thought, *I have to apply everything that I've learned when I go into fall camp.*

Back in Commerce, I was excited to be able to compete for the starting job. The year before, I'd been the board holder. I was itching to play, but I knew how beneficial that year had been from a development aspect.

As I mentioned, I had listened to Kobe Bryant and watched a lot of his videos, in which he talked about just being different and being a workhorse. I took that to heart and said to myself, *I'm not going to drink. I'm not going to party. I will not do anything that will negatively affect my end goal. I will study, hang out with my family, and train for football.*

I just kept telling myself, *Anytime somebody, a teammate, anybody asks me to go out to a party, go out and drink, or go do something that I'm not supposed to do, I'm going to the gym, or I'm hitting the field.* That was my mindset.

Nobody knew about that. I didn't want it to become a joke. But I took it seriously. I went out of my way to work out, throw in the net, or do some drills on the field, whatever I had to do. That was my thing. I knew that if I did that—again, small increments over time—for my whole career, my strides would be tremendously bigger than anybody else's.

In fall camp, I was battling it out. I didn't know if I would be the starter or not. I was doing really well, but I still didn't have confirmation. It was hard to be 100% confident when there had always been obstacles. I always had that small doubt in the back of my mind because none of my former coaches had truly ever believed in me.

A week before the first game, the head coach brought me into his office and said, "All right, are you ready to lead?"

"More than ever," I immediately replied. "I'm your guy."

"You're going to be the starting quarterback for this team," he said. "Let's make it happen."

"Coach," I told him, "I promise you that this is the best decision you've ever made."

After that conversation, I went home and told my wife, "They named me the starter." I just bawled. "Thank you. Thank you for this opportunity."

It had hit me—*I'm really doing this.*

This meant everything. It was the result of my hard work paying off. People pray and work their tails off from a very young age for an opportunity to be a starting quarterback in college, and I was able to do that.

However, I knew that I only had one guaranteed game as a starter. My job was not secured. I had to prove myself every single day, every single practice and game.

Our first game was against a really good football team. We took a bus to Delta State in Mississippi, they had a quarterback who had been a Harlon Hill finalist (the Division II equivalent of the Heisman Trophy) the year before. Everybody kept talking about that quarterback: "We've got to shut this quarterback down. He's the guy we have to be careful of." I remember thinking, *I'll take care of that. We're going to outscore this guy.*

My whole family came to the game. Everybody flew in from California. I remember the first play like it was yesterday. We called a naked play, and they brought the nickel off the edge. They blitzed. Right when I turned around, there was a guy right in my face. I was able to dodge him, and I broke the tackle and threw a 20-yard pass.

I thought, *All right, we're rolling,* and after that, I never looked back.

We had a phenomenal game. *I drove, drove, threw a touchdown pass, scored.* Our defense got a stop. *Drove, drove, drove, ran it in for a touchdown.*

We were firing on all cylinders. I think I only might have missed five passes that entire game, and I threw for two touchdowns and over three hundred yards. I had one of the best games of my career, and it was just the first game.

We went to the locker room, and I just sat there, trying to soak it all in—*what had just happened?*

After that first play, I hit the zone. It's something that you can't understand fully unless you've lived it. Nothing matters at that moment besides executing the play to the best of your ability.

You can't slack for one play. That laser focus has to be in every single play because one of three plays changes every game, right? You drop a snap, you fumble, they pick it up, they score, or you're not locked in with your read, and you read the wrong side and force the ball, and they pick it. You have to be locked in at all times.

I was in that zone, and it never went away. I was completely locked in, and we just dominated the whole game. That win put us on the map because they were a highly ranked team.

My teammates were so excited for me and what was to come. They knew how hard I worked. They knew the passion. They knew the work ethic. But they didn't know how I was going to perform.

A lot of people work hard, but it doesn't necessarily mean that they're good. You have to put everything together and apply your work ethic in the right areas. Somebody can have a lot of work ethic in the weight room, but if it doesn't translate to their position or what they're doing, it's not as beneficial as it might be otherwise.

It's one thing to work hard at something you like and another thing to work hard at something you don't like. That's where you make the biggest strides. I love going out and throwing routes. I can do that all day. However, I've never really loved working out in the weight room.

I did it because I had to, but it wasn't one of the things I loved. I knew that if I put that same passion that I had for throwing the ball and throwing to my guys into the weight room, I was going to be a completely different player, so I did it.

After that first game, I started to think, *I can really do this.*

My family, too, said, "We know you can do it," and I was ready to prove them right.

My wife was so supportive. She went to every single game, drive, or fly, no matter how far away it was. She would also go to all my practices, rain or shine. She went to everything, and I mean everything. It didn't matter if she had homework, an essay due, or a project; she was always there.

I knew that we were in it together. One of the biggest things that I realized was that my journey would be really hard to do alone. Most of the lessons that I've learned and the success that I've had have all been possible because of my relationships and support system.

I want to emphasize that—you have to have a team behind you. Every successful person has had a strong support system, with people around them to help, guide, and build them up along the way.

That year, I just dominated. Week after week, I'd have three or four touchdowns and throw for three hundred yards.

Finally, we got to our last game and had a chance to win the conference. People kept asking me, "Are you nervous? Are you nervous at all? We've got to win this game to win the conference and go to the playoffs."

Whenever someone asked me that, I'd think, "I never get nervous before games." Then I started digging deeper and unpacking everything, and I found out that nerves really come from being unprepared.

If you're prepared and you feel like all your teammates are prepared, there's nothing to be nervous about. There was a lot of excitement—I was excited to get out there, play, and show everyone the work I'd put in all week. I wanted to leave it all on the field.

Yeah, there was excitement, but I never felt nervous. When I talked about that with some teammates, they said, "That's so true."

If I'm prepared, and I'm watching film, and I know what to expect, and I trust everything I put in all week, I trust the coaches, what game plan they have this week for me, and I trust my preparation, I know that there's nothing to worry about. There are no nerves; there's nothing to be nervous about.

I had a great game. I mean, I threw for four hundred yards and four touchdowns, and we absolutely blew out this really good team and won the conference. We were so excited; we were going to the playoffs and hosting because we were a higher seed.

So, we hosted Colorado Mesa. Again, everyone asked me, "Are you nervous?"

"No," I'd answer, "this is what we want. This is what we're here for."

The coaches put a great game plan together, and I dominated, making completion after completion, running the ball, escaping the pocket, and throwing on the run. We beat them and got our first playoff win in school history.

The next week, we were playing Grand Valley State, one of the better Division II schools in the country. They were good every year and had won national championships.

I remember what it felt like to win and what it felt like to lose—and the pain from the losses was much greater than the enjoyment I got from the wins. Every time I got a win, I was like, "Okay, on to the next game. We won; that's what we're supposed to do." But when we lost, it really stung. Eventually, I changed my perspective, turning losses into lessons. I came to realize that you can gain something from every loss and learn something from it. However, going into that next game, I did not want to lose. I wanted to make sure we won.

We went up to Grand Valley State. It's late November or early December, and it's in Michigan, so it's freezing. We were not used to cold games. In fact, that was the first really cold game I had ever played in. When the other team walked out onto the field, we were like, "These guys look like grown men out here." They were huge.

The game started, and we had to fight for every yard. I was making five-yard completions. The separation between the receivers and the DBs got a lot smaller. I had to make tight throws, which meant I had less time to throw. They were completely dominating us.

After we lost that game, I remember thinking, *These guys are the standard of Division II football. This is what we need to look like.* And that was when I set a new standard for what I needed to accomplish and what it would take to become a Division II National Champion.

Lone Star Conference Champion

So, I took some time to go back and reflect on the whole season. We had a great year. We won the conference championship and had the most wins in school history. For the first time in history, we won a home playoff game. But that didn't satisfy me. That wasn't enough in my book.

I had a national championship in mind, and I wanted to win it. I also wanted to win Player of the Year. All those people who believed in me, I wanted to prove them right.

Going into the next year, every single ounce of my body, every time of the day, was going to be aimed toward the goal of winning that national championship.

TODD DURKIN – STRENGTH AND CONDITIONING COACH, MOTIVATIONAL SPEAKER, AND BEST-SELLING AUTHOR

Luis would come out during his off-season breaks when he was in college.

I'd have Drew Brees, Aaron Rodgers, all those guys on the field with all the NFL wideouts, and Luis would come out. He was in college, and I was kind of mentoring him, and I wanted to expose him to the NFL quarterbacks. But it started really way back in the day, just with him coming out to the field. He was always looking to hone his craft.

Training with Todd Durkin

The other thing that I was impressed with was his discipline and his desire to learn. What always enamored me, I had him on my podcast a couple of years ago. And I didn't even know until he did that that he didn't even play high school football. He was a bowler, right? So, I'm like, "How the heck did you not play high school football and then learn?" He went to Southwestern College, where my wife teaches, and he was the ninth-string quarterback. And by the third or fourth week of the season, he was starting, which was a pretty amazing story because of his football IQ, and he was able to grow in a great way in a short period of time.

He played at Southwestern, which led him to Texas A&M Commerce.

He's self-taught in the sense that he's immersed himself around some really great players. So, he trained whenever these guys were training. He'd be there either in the weight room at my gym or on the field, learning and picking brains.

He'd be watching how those guys conduct themselves, how they speak, and their body language. He would always be asking Drew or the other guys about specific football plays as a quarterback, how he would read defenses, and how he prepared. So, it went beyond YouTube; I would say it's pretty hard to learn just by watching YouTube.

I think the consensus is he was always learning. He was immersed in learning, and he found ways to be around other great players. And if you watched him on the field, even when he didn't have a name, you'd be like, "Who's that guy?" Because he's got a cannon of an arm. No one would know who he is, and he'd have a stronger arm than Drew, Chase Daniel, or the other guys out there.

I can't stop thinking that he was a bowler in high school. He went from bowling to baller.

I think the big thing with him is he has got a very keen sense of learning. He puts in the effort, and he's always taking notes. He asks inquisitive questions.

It's not just, "Hey, I want to be the biggest and the strongest." It's from the mental component because your mental processing speed at an elite quarterback level is what differentiates a lot of guys. I mean, you could be six foot four, 240, but that doesn't mean you're going to be a great quarterback. I think at that level, the processing speed is good.

And when you're getting to see a guy like Brees prepare and how he mentally watches film and does all his film work and how he knows his personnel—he'd fly all his guys out, and he knew which guys did what and what they preferred. I think he really studied the nuances of the game, and he's put himself in a situation where—I mean, it really is such an underdog story how he's gotten so far already. He is the kind of guy everyone wants to pull for because he's the underdog. He's not your prototypical guy who did well in high school, went to a big Division I school, and got NIL money.

This guy came out of nowhere, a junior college, ninth-string, bowler in high school, to go into a Division II college and just a man of humility and pure desire to be great in his craft. I mean, he just, he's got resilience; he's got toughness.

If there's one thing, it's that he just keeps showing up. He just keeps showing up, and then he'll call and say, "Hey, where are those guys throwing at?" They're like, "We're throwing at this field." He'll be there. And if he's not throwing that day, he wants to learn.

I would say that would be something that's of note. His story is going to have a big impact. So, I'm glad that he's taking on writing this book because there is not one path to success—whatever you want to do in life—and I think that his story is just a great example of that.

And it's been a ride. I mean, I don't know what's going to happen. I'll tell you this: if he ever goes into the world of coaching, he's going to be one heck of a coach.

I've found that some of the best coaches in the world weren't All-Pro or MVP-caliber players—things may have come more naturally for those guys. Here's a guy who had to work his tail off for decades to get to where he's at. So, if and when he goes into coaching someday, he's going to really be something.

I think that lesson transcends business. I think it trends into his marriage, his family, and his life.

And again, you hear about that now, a guy like Kurt Warner, who used to stock shelves at the grocery store, went to the arena football, got spotted. That's where Luis is at with his thing. I mean, he's just a snap away from being a household name.

FIVE
THE PAIN AND GLORY OF PLAYOFFS

Every ounce of my body was committed to doing everything possible to win a championship. That year, the championship game was going to be in Kansas City.

We had plans to go back to California for the holidays, but I thought, *I need to go to Kansas City. I want to see the atmosphere. I want to see what that's like to play in a championship. I want to see the teams.*

I really wanted to be there at that moment so that when we got there the next year, it was not foreign to me. I'd be able to say, "I've already been here. I've been to the stadium. I know what it's like." I could also tell all the guys what it was like so that when we got there, no one would be surprised, and everyone would be ready to rock.

I told my wife that I wanted to go to Kansas City, and she said, "That's a ten-hour detour from our drive to California."

"What, so you can study ten hours more?" she joked.

I just laughed because she knew we were going to study the whole way there. We ended up bargaining, and I agreed to wash dishes for the next few weeks in exchange for us to go.

She agreed, "All right, fine. Let's go." So, we packed our bags and our pets, and said, "Let's rock and roll."

Now, one thing I didn't tell my wife was that they were supposed to have a snowstorm, and it was going to be around negative ten degrees with windchill. It was also supposed to snow during the game. I didn't tell her that part because I knew that it would be a definite no if I did.

As we approached Kansas City and the weather got colder, she looked up the forecast and said, "It looks like it's about to snow."

"Well," I replied, "we're so close. Let's just keep going. We'll figure it out." So, we drove in a blizzard just so we could watch the championship game.

As luck would have it, one of the teams playing would be our opponent for the first game of the next season. I thought, *This is perfect. I get to go to the next championship game, and I get to watch a team that we're about to play and scout them.*

By the time we arrived at the stadium, about five inches of snow had fallen, and it was freezing. Hardly anyone was at the game because of the brutal cold.

I sat there with my notepad and pen, taking notes throughout the entire game, mentally recording everything about the other team and the production. I wanted to capture it all—I wanted everyone to see what it was like. I soaked it all in, but my wife and I froze our tails off.

I took a lot from that. I remember calling my head coach and telling him with certainty that we were going to be there next year, and I promised him that.

Afterward, we got in our car and drove all the way to California. Again, I studied the whole way there. I wanted a national championship more than anything. That was all I thought about, all I prayed about.

Back home, I trained with Todd Durkin again. He put me through workouts, and I felt like I was in the best shape I'd ever been in.

After the holidays, we drove back to Texas, and I played some good spring ball. I mean, there were some days when the ball never hit the ground. We just felt so good as a team; the team chemistry was there. Everything was amazing. I thought, *We're going to win this. We can really do it.*

Now, we did have a lot of younger guys on the team, and a lot of guys had graduated the year before. So, we had a young group. I knew that I had to get all those young guys on board. I had to teach them the way with work ethic and what it really took.

It started off as two or three guys staying after practice, then five or six. Next, the whole offense wanted to stay after practice. This was followed by the defense staying after. It got to the point where, after our team practices, we would all just go out there on the field on our own, running through drills and plays.

I said to myself, *This is what it takes. This is right here. This is what it takes to be a champion.*

This is the year.

I wrote all my goals on the fridge: national championship, Harlon Hill winner, X amount of touchdowns, no interceptions, no turnovers, being a leader. I had all of these written on my fridge so that I saw them every single day, and I prayed about them every day, too.

I thought about it. I manifested it. This was my obsession.

———

In California for the summer I was excited to get to spend time with Drew Brees again. He had seen all the success I'd had, and we talked about it. I was so thankful for being able to connect with him—to be in the presence of greatness.

That's one of the things where you don't know what you don't know. You can have an image of what greatness is, but until you're around it every day, you don't truly understand what it looks like. This is the blueprint. This is what I need to be. So, being with him for a couple of months before the season was tremendous in terms of my success.

Finally, fall camp came around again, and we were just lighting it up on all cylinders. The ball did not hit the ground during practice sometimes. We were just like, "Nobody's going to stop us."

Our first game was against the championship runners-up, and I wasn't nervous at all—I was excited and ready to go. I just wanted to get out there and play.

They had a really strong team, so this was a big test for us.

We went out there and drove the ball, fighting for every yard, every inch, just like against Grand Valley. It was a low-scoring game, with us chipping away, chipping away, chipping away with a couple of first downs and then *punt, punt, punt.*

It got to the point where I started thinking, *We're not moving the ball. I have to do more. I can do this.*

I started doing things I don't normally do—and I threw an interception. *Oh, my gosh.* Then I threw another. *Oh, no.* And then a third. We were still in the first half.

Keep in mind, I had written on my fridge that I didn't want to throw more than five interceptions all season, and here I was, already at three in the first half of the first game.

I asked myself, *What is going on here?*

We fought for every inch and finally got a field goal, but then they scored a touchdown, so we were down 7–3. In the fourth quarter, we punted the ball to them. Our punter did a great job of pinning them back, so they were inside their own five-yard line. On third down, our defense blitzed and got a safety, making it 7–5.

We were still down and continued to fight for every yard. Near the end of the game, with 30 seconds left, they punted the ball to us. I threw a few completions and got us in field goal range with three seconds left, and we kicked a field goal as time expired, defeating the championship runners-up 8–7.

That game was a real shock to me. I had to dig deep and think about what had just happened. I had gone from the ball not hitting the ground in practice to fighting for every single inch. It was so tough getting anything going that day.

I remember thinking, *This is what a team win is. This is the definition of a team win. Our special teams pins them back. Our defense gets a safety. We're able to finally pull a drive together at the very end and kick a field goal to win the game.*

That showed me the importance of relying on your teammates and just doing your job. You don't have to do anything more or less. Just do your job and trust that everybody else around you is going to do theirs, and that was huge for me.

For weeks two through five, I was lights out. Three touchdowns, no picks. Three touchdowns, no picks. Three touchdowns, four touchdowns, no picks. We were 8–0 and going against another undefeated team, Midwestern State.

We were on our high horse and ready to go. I hadn't thrown an interception since week one. Midwestern was in our conference, so we really wanted to show them that we were the top dog.

But once the game started, everything that could go wrong did. It was absolutely crazy how this game went.

First drive, strip for a touchdown.

Second drive, block punt for a touchdown.

Third drive, I threw an interception, and they ran it back to the five-yard line.

I remember looking up in the second quarter and seeing that we were already down 28–0. Thankfully, we scored right before halftime, making it 28–7 at the break.

During halftime, I told the guys, "We have a chance to do something really special right now. This is an opportunity to show everybody that we can put it all together. We are a complete team, and we can go out there and dominate in the second half."

Sure enough, we came out in the second half, and it was *score, score, score, score.* Soon, it was 47–42. So, we were catching up. I played lights out in the second half, but they ended up getting one last first down and running the clock out.

After the loss, I told myself, *Maybe we needed this.* With every loss, there comes a lesson.

That week of practice, everybody had been just a little too relaxed for my liking and joking around a little too much. We were undefeated and thought that nobody could stop us. We had beaten the championship runners-up and were on our high horse, and that attitude led to a loss.

At our next meeting, I told everybody, "This loss is the result of our wins getting to our heads and joking around in practice and thinking we're all this and that. We have to prove it every single day. We have to prove it. It doesn't matter if you're 10–0 and you lose in the first round of the playoffs. That's pointless. The season would be a disaster, in my opinion, because the goal is a championship."

We ended up winning out and barely making it to the playoffs. Also, that year, they named me conference player of the year. I was fired up about that, but my goal was to win a national championship.

For our first game, we had to go up to Winona State, which had one of the best defenses in Division II football. We dominated that game. Our defense played really well, and the offense was clicking on all cylinders, just like we expected.

On the last drive of the game, we had to get a few more first downs to ice it. They had an All-American safety, a guy who was really good. On one play, I escaped the pocket and was running for a first down. I tried to jump over this safety, and his helmet hit me right on my knee. I spun and hit the turf.

I thought, *Okay, this is fine. I'm good,* but when I got up and tried to walk, my knee buckled. *Oh, boy. This doesn't feel right.*

We got the first down, and then we ran the ball a few more times and were able to ice the game. After the game, I talked with the trainer, and he started doing all these tests on my knee. When he got to the MCL test, my knee went sideways, and I felt excruciating pain. "Did that hurt?" he asked.

"Yeah," I said.

"I can't feel your MCL," he said.

On the flight back home, I remember thinking, *I was able to finish this game, so I'll be fine. I'll be able to play next week.* But by the time we landed, my leg was so stiff and swollen that I couldn't walk or straighten it.

I went to the training room the next day, and they did an MRI and other tests. Afterward, they told me that I had completely torn my MCL. I could either have surgery to repair it, or I could wait a couple of weeks and let it heal on its own.

I said, "I don't have the luxury of waiting a couple of weeks. We're in the second round of the playoffs. There's no way I'm not playing in this game. We have to figure this out."

I went home and did my own research on MCLs, and everything said surgery or six to eight weeks of recovery if you don't get surgery.

"You have to be kidding me," I said. "Like, this is not happening right now."

The offensive coordinator brought me into his office and said, "We're going to go with our second QB to start this week," and I just remember being distraught. I'd gotten us all this way, and now I couldn't even help the team get past the second round.

I just remember asking God, "Why? Why is this happening to me? What's going on? Why now?"

I was devastated and thought my career was over. I wouldn't win a national championship. I wouldn't win Player of the Year. For a Division II player to even get a shot at the NFL, you have to at least win a championship or win the Harlon Hill trophy, and at that point, all I had was a conference championship and conference player of the year.

I went to the rehab room three, four, five times a day, just rehabbing and icing, and I slept with my leg up. My wife massaged my knee, trying to get all the fluid out. I was doing every single thing possible to get ready, but I could still barely even walk. How was I going to play?

By Thursday, it was feeling a little bit better, but I could barely jog—and as for moving laterally, I was done. So, the trainer said, "Let's order you a brace, and we'll ship it to the hotel in Central Washington." That was where we were playing next. "Let's just see how you feel with a custom brace."

We flew to Central Washington, and once there, I put the brace on, took some pain medication, and started jogging. I couldn't cut, but I wanted the coaches to put me through a little workout to see if I was able to play. I did the workout, and I crushed it. I still felt pain, but I wasn't going to tell them that.

Finally, they told me, "We're going to make a decision on whether you're going to play or not in the morning."

Needless to say, I couldn't sleep that night. I ended up falling asleep at four in the morning.

When I woke up a few hours later, the coach called me to his room and told me, "You got us here; I'm going to let you rock and roll. So, let's do it."

"Thank God," I said. "This is the opportunity." I taped my knee up like no other. I had the brace on, and I even taped over it.

We were playing an undefeated team, and it was raining and cold. I thought, *I've got to leave it all out there.*

When I got onto the field, I couldn't move. On the first drive, I missed a few passes, and I thought, *Should I really be out here?* On the next drive, I threw an interception, and then, on the next one, I threw another one.

At this point, my coach came up to me and asked, "Are you going to keep going?"

"Yes, I'm fine," I said. "Let me go out there again."

We had one more drive before halftime. I knew I couldn't let my team down. We had to win the championship, and there was no way

I was coming out, so I went out there for one more drive, and of course, I threw another interception. It was by far the worst first half of my season, but there was no way I was giving up. I was in excruciating pain.

We were down 28–7 at halftime, just like we had been against Midwestern when we had lost; it was the same exact thing. Now, we didn't win against Midwestern, but I knew that we had the opportunity to possibly win because we had almost come back in that game. I knew what we were capable of.

I told the defense, "If they don't score, I promise you, we're going to come back and win." I had thrown three interceptions in the first half, so I was not playing well. I couldn't move around. When the second half came around, I said, "I've got nothing to lose. I don't care about anything else besides trying to win this game."

So, I blocked out all the pain and just started completing passes, and we just kept scoring: drive, drive, score, drive, drive, score, drive, drive, score. Soon, it was 27–27.

The other team scored, leaving us without a minute left to drive and tie the game to go to overtime. I huddled all the guys on the sideline and said, "This is our moment. This is our opportunity." I brought all the seniors up and said, "It's up to you. If this is the last game of your college career, it's up to you. We have an opportunity right now to get it done. If every single person does their job to the best of their ability, we will win this game."

We went out and drove right down the field. *Boom, boom, boom, boom, boom.*

We got into the red zone, and on the first down, we ran the ball—nothing.

Second down, I threw a pass—incomplete.

Third down, I threw a pass—incomplete.

Now it was fourth down with three seconds left. This was it. We had to score to tie and go to overtime.

The coach called a perfect play, a little whip route. The receiver ran a great route. The O-line protected. I threw the ball, and *boom,* it hit him right in his chest—*score, touchdown.* The kicker made the extra point, and we were going to overtime.

We were fired up on the sideline. We had all the momentum, and we got the ball first. We drove down the field and kicked a field goal.

Then they got the ball. They drove down the field and kicked a field goal. Now we were in double overtime.

Our defense went out there and got a huge stop. They prevented the opposing team from getting into field goal range, and they missed their field goal. So, all we had to do was get some yards and get in field goal range to win.

Sure enough, I threw one pass, we ran the ball, and then our kicker made a field goal, and we won the game.

Tears filled my eyes. All the emotions from that week just broke loose. After all the buildup, everything that I'd wanted to happen that week happened. As I hugged my wife and family, I thought, *Nothing is ever too big to accomplish.*

All the odds were against me playing in that game, and I had played so badly in the first half. I was in so much pain. But when it mattered most, the team rallied together, and we made it happen to win the game.

When it was over, I said, "We're winning it all. If we can do this, we can do anything."

The next week, my knee got a little bit better. We went up to Minnesota State, Mankato, in December, and it was freezing cold. We dominated that game. They were never up. We just drove, drove, drove, and scored, scored, scored. We ended up winning 31–21.

The next week, they re-seeded the top four teams to see who was going to get a home playoff game. We got the number two seed, which meant we would be playing the number three team—Harding.

We hosted the semifinal game, so Harding came to Commerce. They ran the triple option, which meant that we had to get up on this team early because they rarely passed the ball. They ran the ball fifty to sixty times a game and tried to run out the clock. So, we knew all week that we were going to have limited possessions.

Our emphasis was to be efficient—no three-and-outs. So, we drove and just started dominating. I mean, we were just scoring, scoring, scoring, and our defense was doing its thing. I remember thinking, *We're really going to play in the championship game. We're dominating this whole game.*

On the second-to-last drive, we were *driving, driving, driving.* On a third down, I got sacked and fell on my throwing elbow. I felt a sharp pain, and I thought, *I'll just shake it off.*

I went to the sideline, and the opposing team started running the ball. They ended up scoring, but we were still up. On our next possession, all we had to do was get one or two first downs, and then we could run out the clock, and the game would be over.

Before a drive, I usually get the ball and throw some warmup passes. This time, when I picked up the ball and tried to throw a pass, it fell to the ground.

Whoa, I thought. *What was that?* I looked at my elbow, and I saw a ball the size of a baseball hanging from it. It was moving around so much that I could not throw.

I told my trainer, and he said, "I think you ruptured your bursa sac."

"What does that mean?" I asked.

"Basically, you are going to have a lot of fluid in there," he told me, "so we're going to have to drain it. But it's going to get really inflamed."

I went back out, and luckily, I didn't have to throw a pass. We ran the ball three or four times and ran the clock out. We won the game and would be playing for a national championship.

I kept telling everybody, "We have to finish. We can't just be satisfied with playing in it. We have to win the game."

The next day, I went to the training room, and the trainer checked out my elbow. "This is not looking good," he said.

"What do you mean, it's not looking good?" I asked.

"If this fluid doesn't go down by the game, you're not going to be able to play," he said. It was going to be hard to throw the ball.

"No way," I said. "I'm just starting to get better with my knee, and now you're telling me that I might not be able to play because I have a balloon on my throwing elbow?" I just remember thinking, *Please, don't let this happen to me.*

A few days passed. I still couldn't practice, and the swelling wasn't going down. I slept with my arm up, trying to get all that fluid to drain down. I went to the training room and drained it a few times, but there was still fluid there, and I thought, *Please let this go away.*

On the Thursday before the game, it felt better, but I didn't know if I would be playing because I hadn't practiced. And practice is everything to me. I wanted to be out there so badly to practice because your preparation and practice are what give you the confidence to be able to succeed in games. When you don't practice, you wonder, *Am I prepared?* You can only do so much off the field, but there's nothing like actually practicing, going against a defense, throwing the football.

On Friday, it was even better, though still not a hundred percent. That was also the day of the Harlon Hill Trophy ceremony. I knew I was a nominee, but I didn't know if I was going to win the award.

Every year, everybody watches the ceremony, and they make this big announcement of who's won the Harlon Hill Trophy.

They announced all the nominees, including me, and I thought, *This is cool, but if I'm going to put everything into one goal, it's going to be a national championship. I just want to win a championship. I don't want to lose.*

I remember looking at the screen and them saying, "The winner of the Harlon Hill Trophy is Luis Perez." The whole team gathered around me and jumped on me. They had my back and were so excited for me.

I thought about everything that I'd gone through, all the adversity, all the lessons I'd learned through the losses, everything I'd learned from Drew Brees, Todd Durkin, and Akili Smith. It was all paying off. The reward was me winning this award.

I can forever say I'm a Harlon Hill Trophy winner—I was the best Division II player in the country that year.

Harlon Hill Trophy

That's an incredible feeling because only my family, my closest friends, and I truly knew the hard work and sacrifices it took to get there.

But all I cared about was one thing: *championship, championship, championship.*

Everything was great, but I couldn't be too happy because I was still dealing with my elbow. *God,* I thought, *I want to enjoy this moment, but I can't because I'm trying to figure out what is going to happen.*

Finally, game day arrived. That day, my wife and I received our bachelor's degrees. Because we were in Kansas and couldn't walk at our college ceremony, the team hosted all football graduates and gave us our diplomas. It was a pretty special moment, a proud moment to be with all of my close family, friends, and teammates and experience it together.

My elbow was slightly better, so I tried throwing. *Okay, this is doable. I think I can do it.* They taped it up and put a compression sleeve over it. Then I said, "Let's do this! It's go time!"

I zoned out. *Boom, boom,* completion after completion, *big play, touchdown, boom, boom, touchdown, touchdown.* The game got out of hand pretty quickly, and our defense was playing lights out, too.

In the fourth quarter, we ran a trick play and scored, and now we were up two or three touchdowns. I thought, *We did it.* Then, in the back of my mind, I said, *Keep going. You can't stop until the clock hits zero.*

Our defense got another stop, and we got the ball back. All we had to do was get one first down. We handed off to our running back, who broke two tackles and got the first down. Everybody knew we had won. The whole sideline erupted. I was so happy. And that was it. We took three knees and won the championship.

2017 Division II National Champions

I just remember celebrating with my teammates, my coaches, and my family and thinking that I had done everything I wanted to do. There's no better feeling than accomplishing what you sought out, prayed about, and wanted to do. It was a surreal feeling.

The first thing that came to mind when I woke up the next day was: *All right, what's next?* I just reflected. I had all my goals on the fridge. Everything I wanted to do in college football, I had done. I was able to overcome so much. The leaders on the team and the team bonding made it happen.

Again, none of it would have happened without my support system. So many things had to happen for me to do what I did and win the championship and the Harlon Hill trophy.

I celebrated for a couple of days. After that, I said, "That's behind me. That door is now closed. I did what I had to do in college football. Let's turn the page. Now, what's my next step to get to the NFL?"

COLBY CARTHEL – HEAD COACH, TEXAS A&M UNIVERSITY-COMMERCE (2013-2018)

I probably didn't give him enough credit when we first recruited him, obviously. The story of him not playing high school football and then going to junior college, learning to play quarterback by watching YouTube videos, and all that will be, I'm sure, well documented, but I'll kind of pick it up, just where we found him at his junior college, Southwestern Junior College, and we recruited him.

Coach Matt Storm and Kevin Blau were out there and kind of met with him at the JC, and then we brought him on a visit. After spending a weekend with him on an official visit, we were kind of talking, and we just fell in love with the guy, who he was, the type of leader he was, and this was our synopsis after all of that: the recruiting process.

We said, well, this guy probably is not an NFL quarterback, but he's the kind of quarterback you can win a national championship with just because of his leadership and who he was, and it just poured out of him—winning did.

Come to find out, we were half right: he was a national-championship-winning quarterback, and he was good enough to play professionally. So, we brought him out and scholarshipped him, and he was still maturing and growing as a quarterback, and we actually redshirted him his first year there at Texas A&M Commerce, which I think really helped him to develop and continue to grow. Just the way he attacked that year was unbelievable.

I mean, he still took every rep, stood behind the quarterback in every drill we did, the starter and the backup, just so he made the most of every snap that he had during that year. And then, obviously, it's well documented, his success. We went two rounds deep his junior year, and then his senior year, he led us to the national championship, won the Harlan Hill, which was the player of the year, and across the country in Division II football, and then, again, continued to be determined, get better, and improve his game.

He is a guy who will not be denied. He has proved the doubters wrong at the junior college level, and he did it at college, and now he's done it at every level of professional football. So, speaking to his determination and work ethic, there was never a stone left unturned in terms of being the very best that he could be, and I'll speak back to that redshift freshman year.

So, he's redshirting. He's not playing in games; he just practices, and then we go to the playoffs, and we're playing up in Michigan, playing Ferris State, and you're limited to a travel roster, and obviously, he's not playing, so he's not on the travel roster.

Well, he hops in a pickup with two guys on the team, and they drive themselves through a blizzard all the way up to Ferris State—I can't remember the town that Ferris State's in—to watch us play, just so he could experience the playoffs and know what it takes and be ready for next year. I mean, who does that as a third-year college student, hop in a pickup and drive across the country in a blizzard just to watch a foot-

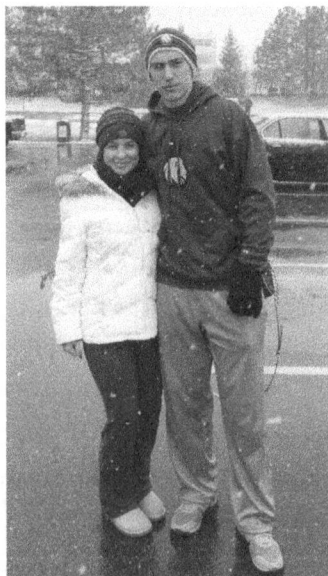

Ferris State

ball game? But he just wanted that experience, and that paid off for him because, again, look at where he ended up.

I think his overall record was 6–1 in playoff games when it came to it, and again, speaking to his determination and work ethic, the very next year, we got beaten in the second round of the playoffs by Grand Valley State up in Michigan.

Fast forward about three weeks. It's the middle of December, the semester is ending, and we're up there watching film as coaches of recruits. It's right at the end of the semester, and Luis pops in to say goodbye.

He's going home for Christmas, and we're in Commerce, Texas, and he's married, and he and his wife, Brenda, they're going back to San Diego, but he says, "We're going to go to the national championship, we're going to Kansas City first."

I'm like, "That's eight hours in the wrong direction, Luis."

And he said, "I know, but I wanted to watch the national championship game because I want to see what it's like. I want to experience it. I want to go. For the past month, I've done all the dishes and done all the chores. Brenda made me a deal that if I do all this stuff, we could go there, and so we're driving there to watch the game, and then we'll go home to San Diego."

So, that sucker and his wife, and again, they're college kids—they ain't got no money—but he drives eight hours east to that national championship game when he should be going west, back to San Diego.

I remember watching it from home, and Luis was texting me, and there was a blizzard there—again, six inches of snow. He's watching Northwest Missouri and North Alabama playing that game, and he called me from one of the stadium tunnels.

"Coach, we can do this. I've been watching them, and I know what it takes, and we can beat them, and I watch these players go by, and we got to work, we got work ahead of us, but we can do this, we can win a national championship."

And I was like, "Golly, this guy's more dedicated than I am. I'm the head coach."

That spoke to who he was, his determination, his work ethic, leaving no stone unturned. He went on and started studying the footballs that were used. Everybody plays with different brands of football, and he's like, "We need to get rid of the GSTs. We need to use the Wilsons, the red footballs, the thousand ones." He had done the research, and nine of the previous ten national champions had played with what we called "red footballs," the thousand ones,

I said, "Luis, if that's what we need to do, we'll do it."

So, I changed our equipment order, canceled the balls we had ordered, and ordered all Wilson GST, or Wilson thousand ones, the red footballs. I mean, every day in practice, he'd throw those balls. "Ah, these are good footballs. We're going to win a national championship," and he just spoke it into existence.

Those are just things that come to mind when talking about his determination, his work ethic, just pushing himself and everybody around in the entire program to heights never thought possible.

I think that he's continued to develop and grow, and he's just not going to be denied. You look at him, and he doesn't look spectacular, and I don't mean that in a bad way, but I mean, he doesn't walk through the door, and you're like, "Oh, my gosh, look at that freak athlete." He's just an average-looking guy, but he just wills himself.

This is kind of a funny story, but he weighed, I don't know, 240 pounds when he came to us, so I was like, "He's kind of chunky," and I said, "Well, Luis, you're from California, and you're shaped like a pear, so I'm going to call you Pearcado," so that was his nickname.

I'm sure that was offensive to him, but we always teased. We had a great relationship, but I called him Pearcado, and he said, "What do I need to weigh?" Bam, I mean, he went to work and lost the weight and just completely changed his body composition,

That's just one of a hundred stories of how he is going to do whatever it takes to give himself the best opportunity to be the very best he can be, which leads you to be a pro. I've always told people the best football players on the planet, they're not always playing in the National Football League;

they're beating the streets or locked up in jail or whatever. They always had roadblocks, excuses, and reasons why they didn't achieve, but the NFL is full of the best football players who are also professionals. They're pros, and that's where Luis is, just a pro in everything that he does.

He was a player I was close with and spent a lot of time with. He's the leader of the team, so again, I try to spend as much time with those guys as I can and just get a feel, and he and I had a professional relationship. We had a friendship relationship. I'm a players' coach. It's a badge that a lot of people look down their nose at, but I think every coach should be a players' coach. That's why we're in this business.

Anyway, I developed a strong relationship with him. We had a players' lounge. It was just outside my office, there in our team room. We had a pool table, and his first year there, he'd come up to visit with me in the office, or I'd see him, and we'd end up playing pool and, just talking about life, the football team, the program, whatever came up, just spending time together.

One game of pool turned into two, which turned into three, and I mean, it got to where, again, he's a very competitive person, and so am I, and so we got to where we'd compete pretty good, playing pool.

That first year there, I beat him like nobody's business. I'd beat him four out of every five games at least, and then he went home one time, I think it was over Christmas or summer break or whatever, and he came back, and all of a sudden, he starts hitting these bank shots, I mean, those are tough shots to make on a pool table, "Holy mackerel, that's the third time you've banked something. What in the world? You've been practicing."

He said, "Oh, coach, I was tired of getting beat, so I started watching YouTube videos on how to play pool and how to get better at these bank shots."

He was night and day better, and that goes back to exactly how he taught himself to play football. He's a bowler in high school, decided he wanted to play football, goes to junior college, and watches YouTube videos on how to play quarterback.

Now, here we are, four years later, and he's playing pool with his head coach; he's getting his tail whipped, and he doesn't like it, so he again turns back to YouTube to learn how to be better at pool and starts making all these bank shots.

His senior year, during the fall semester—I'm embarrassed to say this, but I think we kept records—I think we played over 250 or 300 games of pool, and that's just how much time we spent together.

His first year there, I was beating him four out of every five games, but that last semester he was there with us, he was getting a better part of me on the pool table, and that just again speaks to who he is.

I will say this, though. The last time we played, I won, so I think I may retire and be the all-time champion, as he calls it.

SIX
PRO DAY AND NFL DREAMS

Once I closed the chapter on college football, I immediately turned the page and wondered, *What's next?*

In college (back then), you weren't allowed to talk to agents until after the season. So immediately after, NFL agents reached out. I ended up signing with one, and he showed me the ropes. He told me what needed to be done and what it was going to take to make it.

"In about three weeks, you need to start your combine prep," he told me. "You have to find a training facility, find a quarterback coach, and train for about ten to 12 weeks. Specifically, you have to train for your 40, your 5-10-5, your vertical, and your broad jump, and you have to get ready for your pro day. You have to start practicing throwing under center because that's something that you didn't do in college."

I did a lot of research on where I wanted to go, and I knew from talking to a lot of mentors that I didn't want to just be in one spot. I wanted to go to different places to get many different things in my toolbox. One quarterback coach can teach you one thing, and a different coach can teach you another.

I went to this place called XPE in Florida. My knee still wasn't

100% healed, and I was still rehabbing it, but I felt good otherwise. They put me through a drop process, and I fell in love with the quarterback coach. Everything was great. I was there for a few weeks. However, I didn't feel that I was getting the attention that I deserved because they had a lot of big-name guys there.

So after that, I told my agent, "I don't think I'm getting the attention that I deserve. My expectations might be too high. I don't know. But this is not what I'm looking for. I want to go somewhere else."

I reached out to another buddy of mine, Tim Jenkins. He had played in the NFL and had a quarterback school in Colorado. I flew out there and stayed there for about two weeks. He really dug deep with the playbook, terminology, and how NFL teams call plays. I just knew double right 90, and that was it (this was the extent of calls in college). That was the whole play call.

He started implementing all these different plays that were 15 to 20 words long that you had to memorize.

Akili Smith was a big influence in that because he told me, "Everybody can teach you how to throw a football, but if you don't know how to master a playbook and you don't know how to spit out the plays and visualize the plays, you're worth nothing. You can throw the prettiest ball. You'll be the most accurate passer, but if you can't operate an offense and spit out a play call in the huddle, you're not going anywhere." I took that to heart.

Tim Jenkins helped me so much. I was only there for two weeks, but I learned a lot. After that, I said, "I want to go somewhere else. I want to learn from someone else."

I went to a place called Test in New Jersey. Now, keep in mind that my wife was alone while we were there. She was with me the whole way. She traveled with me and helped me throughout the whole process. The days were long but having someone there gave me a sense of security.

In New Jersey, I ended up getting with a quarterback coach, Tony Racioppi. He was a phenomenal coach. He taught me so much, but it was different. With Tim Jenkins, it was more of the playbook break-down. Tony Racioppi's coaching was about footwork, how to use your body, and understanding the biomechanics of being a quarter-back. I learned so much from him.

I also built a great relationship with the trainer there, Kevin Dunn, who was the owner of Test. He took me under his wing. Both Tony and Kevin were super hands-on the whole time, so I spent the majority of my time with them.

The entire time I was there, my agent was telling me, "We have to try to get you into another pro day. Texas A&M Commerce is a smaller school, so you won't get that many scouts there. We have to get you in front of a lot of scouts and position coaches."

I reached out to a bunch of different people. Finally, I texted George Whitefield and said, *"I just finished out my season, just won the Harlon Hill Trophy, won the National Championship, and I'm looking into getting a big-time pro day."*

He texted back, *"Done. I got you into A&M's pro day."*

"Texas A&M? The Aggies?"

"Yep. I know Jimbo Fisher. I just got you to throw. They're looking for a quarterback."

That pro day was four days after my Commerce pro day. So, after training, training, training, and rehabbing, finally, the big day came. I went through my pro day at Commerce, and I killed it.

The guy who ran my pro day was Dustin Vaughn. Well, Dustin had been coached by Coach Carthel at West Texas A&M, who was one of my idols and the reason I went to Commerce. Dustin and I connected. He would come to some of our games and had a great relationship with the coaches. He said, "I just moved to Dallas. Can I help you run your pro day?"

I said, "Absolutely," so he was the one who put together the pro day script. He put everything together for me, all the routes. He made it so simple for me to just go out there and execute. We went through the pro day multiple times, and he helped me make it happen.

I had a phenomenal day in front of a lot of scouts, did my thing, and tested well. My focus now was on A&M. I knew that there would be a lot of coaches there because they had Christian Kirk, Damion Ratley, all these big-time prospects coming out, first- and second-round picks. I knew this was going to be the biggest pro day.

I went to those guys and said, "Do you guys want to practice beforehand?" So, I was able to throw to those guys, and I was excited and ready to go.

I told my agent, "This is going to be it. This is the time. This is my moment to shine and show everybody that I belong in Division I and the NFL."

I got to College Station a few days early, and my agent called me and said, "I just got the word that Johnny Manziel is throwing at the pro day. I don't know if you're going to be able to throw."

"What do you mean?" I said.

"Johnny's trying to make a comeback, and A&M is letting him come throw there at the pro day, so I don't know if you're going to be able to throw. I'll let you know in the morning. I'm going to try to find out some more information."

That night, I thought, *Why? Why is this happening to me? This is my shot. This is it. I mean, this is my dream. I'm throwing at Texas A&M's pro day in front of all these position coaches in the NFL, all these scouts, assistant general managers, and general managers. This is my opportunity.*

The next morning, he called and said, "I just got the word. You can throw with him."

That was a huge relief at first. But then I thought, *This is not ideal. He's going to take all my shine.* Then I switched my perspective and said, "Well, everybody's going to see me throwing with Johnny Manziel, former first-round pick, and Heisman Trophy winner. This is a good thing. Let me go out there and throw side by side with him so they can compare me to him."

I went out there and threw the ball like no other. I was in the zone for ball after ball, just on point. Only two balls hit the ground all day. Johnny Manziel was looking at me like, *Who is this guy? Where did he come from?*

After it was over, Johnny and I were talking, and a bunch of scouts came up to me and said, "Tell me your story." It was a very cool moment. Johnny even put out a tweet that really helped me, put me on the map. He said, *"Just throwing with Luis Perez, phenomenal quarterback, can spin it like no other. Definitely an NFL-caliber quarterback. Excited to see where you land."*

I remember thinking, *I'm a college kid, and Johnny Manziel just tweeted at me. Man, this is just amazing. I'm in the clouds right now.*

Afterward, I went home and thought, *This is great. Position coaches, general managers, and big-time scouts were all there watching me and Johnny Manziel throw side by side.*

Everything in life is perspective.

When I found out Johnny was going to throw, my first thought was that he would take my spotlight. But then I took that "negative" and turned it into a positive, and it ended up being great for me. It couldn't have worked out any better.

My wife and I returned to California, and there was a little dead period between pro day and the draft. I continued to train, getting ready for draft day.

Finally, draft day came around, and we had a party at my uncle's house. Everybody was there, my family and friends; it was a big moment. Only 1% of players make it to the NFL, maybe even less than that, so it was exciting.

I knew I wasn't going to be picked in the first or second round, but there had been some talk that I might be a later-round pick or an undrafted free agent. I thought I might go in the sixth or seventh round.

The draft is broken up into three days. The first day is for the first-round picks. The second day is rounds two through four, and the third day is five through seven. We had the party on the third day because that was when we believed I might get picked.

We were all sitting down on the couch. I had my phone on loud and on the table in case somebody called me. I would get text messages, and everyone would get excited. Then I'd look at it and see that it wasn't a team—it was just a buddy from high school or whatever, wishing me luck.

The fifth round went by, and I looked up at the TV screen and saw a tweet by NFL journalist Chris Mortenson that said something along the lines of, *"Keep an eye out for Luis Perez. Great story. Mel Kiper thinks he could be one of the next quarterbacks taken in the draft."*

Seeing that on national television, I thought, *Oh, my gosh. This is it. Any second now, I'm going to get picked.* We were all ecstatic, but we still didn't know where I would land.

The sixth round went by, and then we were in the seventh round. *Okay,* I thought. *Here it comes.* But then the seventh round passed, and I heard nothing. I didn't get drafted.

Now I was thinking, *Is this it? Is my career done? I didn't get picked. I didn't get drafted.* As a kid, your dream is to hear your name called when you get drafted.

I left the party and went for a long, long walk. I was kind of in shock because all these people had been telling me that I was going to get drafted. I had just won the Heisman of Division II, and I'd won a national championship. I'd broken all kinds of records. I'd done everything possible at my level. I couldn't have done anything better.

Those thoughts eased me at first, but then I thought, *This is not fair. I need to be given an opportunity.* I asked God, "Why is this happening to me? I don't understand. I did everything I could to be in this position to get an opportunity. I've done everything right."

It was about a two-hour walk. When I got back, I called my agent and said, "What's going on? Are you hearing anything? Are any teams interested? Just give me something, a workout, a tryout."

"I have nothing," he said. "There's nothing."

Then I started thinking, *Did I get the right agent?* I went down a huge rabbit hole of: *What could I have done differently?* I was devastated. My whole family was devastated.

For the next two weeks, I thought, *This is it. I'm done playing football, and I need to start pursuing other things.*

Then my agent called and said, "The Rams are having a local tryout. If you live within a certain distance from the facility, you can get invited. And they just had a quarterback drop out of their local tryout because he got signed elsewhere. Do you want to go?"

"Absolutely!" I said.

Two days later, I flew to LA from San Diego. I thought, *There is no way I am walking out of here without a contract. There's no way. There's no way.* I prayed, "Please, God, give me all the power, give me the wisdom, give me the skills, give me everything that I need. Equip me with everything that I need to get through this workout and get signed."

I arrived at camp, and there were five quarterbacks and probably 30 to 40 skilled players, including receivers, tight ends, and running backs. Before the workout, they said, "Probably only three or four of you are going to get signed from this whole workout," and I immediately thought, *The odds are against me here.*

We started warming up, and I was full of adrenaline. All the other guys were Division I quarterbacks. I was the only Division II quarterback there, but I had thrown side by side with Drew Brees and Chase Daniel when training, so I should feel confident.

I thought, *These guys might be better because they're Division I.* That was my thought process back then. *I have to do everything possible to outdo these guys.*

But as we started throwing the ball, I thought, *I really have a chance here.* We were throwing routes, and I was hitting the balls on the money. I probably threw 45 passes, and only one or two hit the ground all day.

After the workout, I was pretty excited and proud of my performance. I remember sitting at the table where everybody was waiting, and they just called people one by one to talk to the general manager, who would tell them their status. I was one of the last ones. I went in, and the GM said, "Tell me your story again."

"I didn't play high school football," I said. "I was going to become a professional bowler..." I told him my story again. I remember telling myself, *You deserve to get a contract.*

"I hadn't planned on signing a QB," he said, and my heart dropped. "We just needed to fill a spot, but you did so well... I'm going to sign you."

I couldn't believe it. I'd done it. The general manager of the Rams had just told me that he was signing me and that he was proud of what I had done. All I could think was: *This is awesome. This is awesome.*

I got signed, and then I immediately called my wife and parents and told them. Back then, I didn't really know how the process worked. I thought, *Okay, you're signed. You're pretty much good. You're on the team.* I didn't know how many people made the roster at the end.

Everybody took a shuttle to the airport, and I was so excited about getting signed. I called my coaches back home. I called my friends and my mentors. I was so distracted that I missed my flight home and had to find another one. For four or five hours, I just sat there in the airport, soaking everything in. Finally, I got on a plane and flew back home.

Once home, I continued training. I had about a week before we had to go back for organized team activities (OTAs). Then I got all my stuff ready, packed everything up, and drove to LA so I could have my car.

On the first day of OTAs, all these high-caliber guys were there: Jared Goff, Todd Gurley, Cooper Kupp, Robert Woods, Brandin Cooks, Aaron Donald—the Rams had some big names.

On that first day of practice, I was starstruck. I was throwing next to Jared Goff and all these guys. Being in the presence of these players felt amazing.

After that first day, I thought, *I can definitely play at this level.* That gave me so much more confidence.

I was trying my best. I knew I could throw with these guys, but being able to listen to fifteen to seventeen words, repeat them, understand them, and get the whole team to understand them in the huddle—that's the biggest thing.

A few days in, I realized that there was a ton of verbiage I wasn't used to. I remember sleeping in my room every night with headphones connected to my tape recorder, listening to all the plays from the day before over and over. All night, I had all those plays repeating in my mind.

I wanted to prove that I could really do it. Again, I didn't care about the people who said, "You can't do it." Instead, I was motivated to prove right to the people who believed in me—my family, friends, coaches, and mentors.

At OTAs, parking was assigned, and each space was numbered. I would get to the facility at 4:30 every morning and not leave until about 8 p.m. I would always be one of the first ones there. I was wearing number nine, so I would park in the ninth spot, and that was it.

Come to find out that those numbers had nothing to do with jersey numbers. All the front-row spots were for coaches or veteran players. Finally, on the last day of OTAs, somebody saw me pulling out of the spot and said, "Hey, that's Wade Phillips's spot." Whoops.

Right after OTAs, the player development guy said, "We're taking a trip to Mexico, and we'd like to send you and your wife out since we'll be playing in Mexico City this year." I found out that Michael Brockers and Eric Dickerson were going.

Oh, wow, I thought. *Eric Dickerson? Hall of Fame running back Eric Dickerson? This was great.*

I went, and we had a blast in Mexico promoting the game. I was also growing closer to everybody. On the flight, I got to sit next to Dickerson and talk to him, and it was an amazing moment.

I thought, *I'm good. Relationships are everything. I'm going to make the team. They're bringing me to Mexico. They chose me and only two other players. This is awesome.*

After the trip, we had about eight weeks in the summer to get ready for training camp. I studied my butt off. I mean, I studied every single day and night. Getting with Todd Durkin again and Drew Brees was crucial. It was also really beneficial getting with Tom and fine-tuning everything.

Drew and I just got closer. It was a good time. I learned a lot from him that summer. I just watched him, observed him, and tried to soak in as much information as I could from him.

I was always thinking, *How can I get an edge? How can I be different from everybody else so I can be better?*

I came up with the idea of my wife coming out to the field with me and holding the iPad with the plays and having her repeat them to me, just like she's a head coach.

Then I thought, *Let me turn it up a notch. Why don't I buy scrimmage vests, called pinnies, with everybody's letter on them, X, F, Y, Z, and have everyone jog routes?*

Going through formations with X, F, Y, Z pinnies

I went to Dick's Sporting Goods, bought pinnies, and taped the letters to the backs of them. Then, I got my friends and family members out on the field so I could visualize all the plays by having them jog through the routes.

We'd be out there for two hours. My wife would hold the iPad, and my family members and friends would stand in a huddle with their pinnies on. Then, my wife would call a play. I would have to repeat it to my buddies, and they would look at the iPad so they knew where to go. Then, they would go to their spots and jog the routes.

That was really beneficial. And I took big strides before going into training camp. You always need to find a competitive edge and be different. So, I did that alongside everything else.

When I got back to training camp, I felt tuned up and ready to go. An article came out, maybe the first or second practice of camp, and it said that Coach Sean McVay was pissed off that I had beaten him to the facility.

I said to myself, *What is this?*

I went back and listened to the interview. In it, the reporter asked Coach McVay, "What do you think about Luis Perez? How's he been doing?"

McVay replied, "You know, I'm a little pissed off. He kind of beat me to the facility."

Now, he was joking, right? But he was talking about my work ethic and the way I approach the game.

Reading that made me excited. I felt like I was finally being seen and that my hard work was paying off. *I'm making this team,* I thought.

I had a great training camp, and the preseason arrived. *I'm going to show the world that I can play at this level,* I told myself. I'd get there at 4:30 in the morning and watch tapes. The first game was against the Raiders, so I was just watching them, watching them, watching them.

One morning, I was in there, and the quarterback coach walked in and said, "Sir, I need to talk to you. We're not going to play you in preseason. You showed us so much in training camp that we don't want you to go out there and play well and have a team take you from our practice squad.

Our plan is for you to be on the practice squad this year and possibly compete for the backup spot next year."

Is this good or bad? I wondered. I really didn't know. But I believed, *Wow, this is great. At least I'm solidified. This is what they're going to do with me. This is great.*

Week two of the preseason goes by, and I don't play.

Week three goes by. I don't play.

They tell me the same thing: "You're not going to play."

Now, I'm really excited because I've figured out what being on the practice team means. I get to learn. I get to develop and be around everybody. I get to be a sponge and soak up everything I can from all these great coaches and players.

Before the fourth preseason game, they brought me in and said, "We might play you a little bit in the fourth quarter."

"Okay, great," I said. "This is awesome."

We were playing the Saints in New Orleans, in the Superdome. Before the game, I was on the field, throwing routes with the receivers, and somebody tapped me on the shoulder. I turned around, and it was Drew Brees.

He pulled me out, and we just talked for about five minutes. It was a crazy moment. He told me how proud he was of me, how he loved my work ethic and was excited to see me play, and how we had to get a picture together after the game. I couldn't believe it.

When I was done talking to him, I went back to the drills, and everybody was looking at me with wide eyes, like, *Whoa, what just happened? Why is Drew Brees coming up to this rookie and talking to him?* Everybody asked me, "Hey, how do you know him?"

I ended up explaining, "He and I have been training together the last couple of years."

We played the game, and I didn't see any action in the first half. In the fourth quarter, they put me in, and we were down a bunch. I threw a few passes and ran the ball, and that was it—it was done. They just wanted me to get my feet wet.

After the game, Drew Brees and I took a picture together and talked a little bit. It was a surreal moment and something I'll never forget. It's just awesome to see somebody as high caliber as him be so humble.

Rams vs. Saints 2018

When we got back home, sure enough, they said, "We're going to put you on the practice squad." I went to the facility, signed the paperwork, and that was that. I was so excited, and my family was, too.

The first week of the season, we played the Raiders. I didn't travel to the game because the practice squad doesn't go to away games. So, I spent my time studying the playbook again, still trying to learn. I was on cloud nine.

We beat the Raiders, and I thought, *This is awesome. We're going to have a good team.* It was a pretty convincing win.

My wife and I had to transition from being in a hotel in training camp to finding our own place, so we were scrambling for an apartment. We finally got one and furnished it. I felt like I was set. We were in a nice spot, and it was great.

Week two came, and we played the Cardinals. It was another convincing win—we dominated. I continued having great practices.

After that game, we had a bunch of injuries. Some offensive linemen had gotten hurt. Our kicker got hurt. Aaron Donald was holding out that year, so he wasn't on the roster yet. I didn't think anything of that. I just remember they were having a lot of injuries.

On our day off, I was headed to a community service event that I had signed up for. The personnel guy called me and said, "The general manager wants to see you." They turned around and took me to the general manager. I didn't know what to expect. I even thought I might be getting promoted.

When I got there, the general manager said, "I really love what you've been doing. You're a phenomenal quarterback. We've had a lot of injuries this week, and we're carrying four quarterbacks right now. Normally, teams only carry three. We're in a position to make a Super Bowl run and are not in a developmental stage right now as an organization, so we're going to have to let you go."

My first thought was, *But I just got an apartment and a year lease. I just furnished the place. You guys told me all year that I'm doing amazing, and now you're cutting me?* I didn't understand what was going on. Like, what went wrong?

I went to my locker, and they gave me a plastic bag. As I put all my stuff in it and removed the nameplate, I kept saying to myself, *Why is this happening to me? Why?* Then I went home and told my wife that I got cut. That was definitely one of the hardest things I had to do early in my pro career.

We just started crying together. A lot of emotions tore through me, including anger and uncertainty. I had been on cloud nine, thinking my dreams were coming true, and now I'd hit rock bottom.

At that moment, I felt like my career was over. I had missed my opportunity. It was gone, and there was nothing else I could do.

Looking back on it now, I should have switched my perspective. You're going to fall many times; the important thing is how quickly you get up and continue to move forward. You can't stay down for too long. And you can always find a positive in every negative situation. That's a given.

It went back to my faith and trusting the process. I wanted to play in the NFL and win Super Bowls. I had all these dreams and aspirations, but I didn't know how I was going to achieve them. The answer is to have faith, trust the process, and just continue to do your part and control what you can control.

I had done everything I possibly could, so I should have felt good about myself. I gave every single ounce of effort that I had. I couldn't have done one thing better. I got there at 4:30 in the morning. I didn't leave till nine. I would only sleep five or six hours at the most. This was every single day. The determination I had to learn the playbook was unmatched. I was obsessed with being the best, telling myself, *I have to be the best, and I need to do whatever it takes to be the best.*

When they told me I was cut, it was hard for me to see that. Instead, all I could think was, *This is it. I'm done.*

Now, however, I can look back and see that everything happens for a reason. You just have to get up, move forward, and try again.

I called my agent and said, "They just released me. What's going on?"

"I'm going to try to get you on another team," he said.

My wife and I stayed in that apartment for a few more weeks, hoping that they would call me back. Keep in mind, I didn't have any film because I had been told that they didn't want to expose me at the moment, so now I was in a lose-lose situation.

Nothing happened, and that was it. So we drove back to San Diego. I had no idea what to do next. My agent told me that he had nothing. He had no workouts lined up.

So, I was back home, clueless as to what to do. Should I get a real job? Was there a chance that I might get picked up? I had no idea.

Then I got a DM from Chris Mortensen.

SEVEN
BALANCING BETWEEN LEAGUES

After getting released, I went back home, and I had no idea what would come next. I thought, *Do I have to get a job?* I just didn't know what to do.

One day, I received a tweet from ESPN NFL journalist Chris Mortensen that said, *"Hey, bud, there's this league called the Alliance of American Football, the AAF, and it's coming up soon. They're playing in the spring. The kickoff is a week after the Super Bowl. You should look into it. My son, Alex Mortensen, is a coach for one of the teams."*

I called my agent and asked him, "What is this Alliance of American Football League?" We did some research and saw that it was funded and had a lot of big names behind it.

My agent said, "Yeah, this is a legit league."

"What's the pay like?" I asked.

"The pay's good, too."

"Okay," I said, "this is good."

It was a new league, and they were trying to figure out the logistics of everything. Would they have the same rules as the NFL?

Ultimately, the rules were a little different. The play clocks were a little shorter, and there was no kicking for an extra point—you could only go for two. There was no onside kick. The onside kick was that you go for it on fourth and 15 at your own 25-yard line. If you got it, your drive continued. If you didn't, the defense got the ball wherever they stopped you.

I thought, *This could be something interesting that I need to look into. I need to play more ball.*

They had a quarterback camp in San Antonio, at the Alamodome, with about two hundred quarterbacks split up into different groups, and my agent got me into that. There were some big-name guys there—Ryan Mallett, Christian Hackenberg, and Dustin Vaughn, one of the guys I looked up to in college.

I thought, *I have to outdo everybody. I am playing from behind. I'm a small school guy. This is my time. I have to get on. I have to play football again. I don't want to go work for my dad or do anything like that.* I just knew I did not want to work a normal 9-5 job. My love and passion was football.

At the camp, I crushed it. I mean, very few balls hit the ground. Afterward, every single GM in the league came to me and asked about my story. "We're going to have a quarterback draft in a few weeks, so be on the lookout and keep training," they said.

My agent called me after and said, "I got a call from a bunch of different GMs. You did a phenomenal job. They're going to hold a draft in Las Vegas in a few weeks, and they're going to draft quarterbacks. They're only going to take the top five quarterbacks, and they're going to invite them to Vegas to be there in person."

I hope I get that call, I thought.

A week or two went by, and I'd heard nothing. Finally, I got a phone call from the director of the league, and he said, "We're all very impressed with what you've done. We've talked to the Rams, and they really like you. They vouched for you. This is a league for a player like you. I want to invite you to the draft in Vegas."

Here it is, I thought. *This is my time.*

At the draft, it was me, Josh Johnson, Christian Hackenberg, and Zach Mettenberger. All of these guys had been starters in the NFL. I was the only guy who was kind of a rookie and didn't really play in the NFL, just a little in preseason.

Nobody knew who was going to get picked first. The San Diego team had the first pick, and they had Mike Martz. Well, Mike Martz is the greatest show on turf, the Rams coach who coached Kurt Warner. Now, at the time, there was some talk about me having a pretty crazy story, similar to Kurt Warner's, so I thought, *This will be great. If I'm the first pick, I'll get to be coached by the same guy Kurt Warner was coached by.*

Before the draft, they did a little segment on me and talked about how I didn't play football in high school. I was the only quarterback they did that for, so that was pretty neat.

The draft started, and Heinz Ward walked up and said, "For the first pick, the San Diego Fleet select... Josh Johnson."

I thought, *Oh, well. I wanted to be in San Diego to be with Mike Martz, but some things just don't always go your way.* My perspective had already changed. I'd already gone through a lot, so I was just thinking, *There's a positive in every situation. I may not know what it is at the moment, but I know there's a reason I didn't get picked.*

The second pick came, and I didn't get picked. The third pick came, and I didn't get picked. Fourth pick, nothing. Then the fifth pick came, and I heard, "The Birmingham Iron select... Luis Perez."

Alliance of American Football (AAF) Birmingham Iron

I was ecstatic. I got drafted. This meant I would get to play for former NFL defensive coordinator Tim Lewis, who's an awesome, awesome guy. I got to be with Alex Mortensen, who is Chris Mortensen's son. Ironically, now we were on the same team, he was coaching the receivers, and I was with the quarterbacks.

(Note: I want to share my condolences with the Mortensen family. Chris Mortensen was diagnosed with Stage IV throat cancer and tragically passed away on March 3, 2024, at the age of 72. He was a respected and loved American journalist, especially in NFL circles.)

Training camp rolls around, and I report. During camp, I dominated, and they were basically telling me, "This is your job. You're doing really well. You're our starting quarterback." Halfway through camp, I already knew I was the guy. I mean, I was killing it.

Our first game of the year was against the Memphis Express. They had a QB who was a second-round pick in the NFL. I thought, *I have to outdo this guy.*

We had a very tight group. We had a lot of veterans on our team and a lot of great leaders who kind of showed me the way and whom I was really close with, guys like Trent Richardson and Quinton Patton. We had a lot of guys who were established in the NFL and were great people and players. So, we were just fired up. I was just anxious and excited to go play. Again, there were no nerves because nerves come from a lack of preparation. I was prepared, and I knew I was prepared.

So we went out there, and on the first play of the game, I threw a completion; our tight end, Braedon Bowman, caught the ball, hurdles a guy, and *boom*, the crowd erupts. A couple of plays later, we *drove, drove, drove,* and scored.

The defense got a stop, and we went out there again and drove, drove, drove, touchdown, drove, drove, drove, touchdown. I mean, we were completely killing it. I was outplaying the opposing quarterback and probably having the most fun I'd had in a very long time. We beat them 26 to zero on opening day.

After the game, I called my agent. "Wow," he said. "You did a phenomenal job. A bunch of teams are calling me."

This is great, I thought. *I'm on the path where I need to be to go back to the NFL.*

We played a few more games and were still undefeated. Our next game was against the Orlando Apollos. They came to us, and they were a really good football team. We went back and forth, and I was not playing so well.

The coach said, "If you don't score on this drive, you're coming out."

What? I thought. Being benched was the furthest thing from my mind. *What do you mean you're going to bench me? We're 5–0, like, what do you mean?*

We didn't score that drive. I threw an interception, and he benched me. I remember thinking, *I just went from a bunch of NFL teams being interested in me to being benched.* I was in a state of shock.

We ended up losing that game. The next week, we were playing San Diego at Qualcomm Stadium. The coach brought me into the office and said, "You should not start this week."

My jaw dropped.

There's no way this is happening, I thought. *I'm going to have probably two hundred people come out to watch me at the San Diego game, and I'm not going to play?*

At practice that week, I didn't get any reps, and I told everybody back home, "Hey, guys, I'm not going to play. You don't have to come to the game." I was devastated because I wanted to prove to my family that I belonged in the NFL and that I could do it for them.

Finally, the day of the game arrived. My family still showed up. I was on the sideline the whole time. During the third drive of the game, the quarterback who was in got hit in the head and fell to the ground. He came off the field, and they rolled him out with a concussion. The coach said, "Luis, you're in."

We were down ten points. On my first drive, I threw a Texas route to Trent Richardson. He trucked past three guys and launched himself into the end zone for a touchdown. The crowd went wild. I looked up at the stands and saw my family. It was a great feeling.

On the next drive, we scored another touchdown. Then they scored, and we started going back and forth, back and forth.

Finally, they were up 32–25, and we got the ball and were driving. There were about four minutes left in the game. So, we drove and got a couple of fourth-down conversions.

In the end, I threw a goal route to Damien Washington, who caught it in the end zone for a touchdown, and we tied the game, 32–32.

Now they got the ball, and our defense stopped them three and out. We got the ball back with a minute left and no timeouts. All we needed was a field goal. I knew that Nick Novak, on the sideline, was licking his chops because he had played for the Chargers and this was his time to shine. He had kicked in the Qualcomm Stadium for years.

I remember thinking, *I've got to score here. I've got to score here.* I just got in the zone again. "It does not matter what happens. All I care about is scoring a field goal right now and driving down the field." So, *completion, completion.* I ran the ball for a first down, *completion, completion.*

There was about 15 seconds left. We had to get out of bounds, but we also needed a few more yards.

My first read was not there.

My second read was not there.

My third read was not there.

I escaped the pocket and rolled out. I got about six yards and then ran out of bounds. There were three seconds left. It was about a 45-yard field goal.

Nick Novak went out there, kicked a field goal right down the middle, and Birmingham Iron won 35–32.

I ran to the stands and saw a whole section where everyone had Perez jerseys on. It was just a cool moment. I hugged my wife and family. It was a great moment—in Qualcomm, down to the wire, and ending with a game-winning drive.

I got the starting job back and felt like I was back on track. We won the next few games, and then we were playing against the Memphis Express again. I remember thinking, *These guys are going to give us their all. They were upset about how we beat them on opening day.*

The week before the game, the league announced that Memphis Express had signed Johnny Manziel. I thought, *There's no way. There's no way Johnny Manziel is playing in my league right now. Heisman Trophy winner, first-round pick. No way.*

Sure enough, it was true. I would be playing against Johnny Manziel. Things had come full circle. I'd thrown with him on Pro Day, and now I would be playing against him in a real game.

Before the game, Johnny and I talked, and he told me how he'd gotten there. All I could think was, *I've got to bring my A game. I'm playing against Johnny Manziel.*

The game started, and in the first drive, I made three 30-yard passes, boom, boom, boom, and we scored. *This is going to be a cake-walk,* I thought.

Second drive, *boom, boom, boom,* score: 14–0.

Now, I was thinking, *Oh, we're good. Our defense is playing great. This is awesome.* Now, keep in mind that Johnny Manziel had gotten there midweek and wasn't their starting quarterback. They had another quarterback starting.

Soon, they were down 17–0 and wanted a spark, so they threw Johnny Manziel in there. He went in and had a 30-yard run, then a 40-yard run, and then scored a touchdown.

Oh, boy, I thought. *Now they have all the momentum. Johnny Manziel just gave them the spark that they needed. Man, we've got to pick it up.*

On the next drive, we scored, and then they scored again, too. Now there was about two minutes left, and we were up 27–14.

All right, I thought, *let's run the ball a couple of times. Let's just run the clock out.*

So, that's what we did. We ran the ball and killed a little bit of clock, and I was on the sideline, thinking, *We're going to win the game.* Then Johnny Manziel went out there, *drive, drive, drive, score.* Now it was 27–21.

It's important to remember that there were no onside kicks. Instead, you got the ball on your own 25-yard line, and it was fourth and 15. If you got it, you kept going. This is what they opted to do.

Manziel threw a pass, and they got a first down. I thought, *You've got to be kidding me.* Now they were driving, driving, driving. As time expired, Johnny Manziel threw a pass for a touchdown, and they tied the game.

Now we were going to overtime. We had Trent Richardson, so we were thinking, *Let's get close enough to run the ball so Trent can get in.*

We got the ball first and drove down the field, then had a good run by Trent. On fourth down, we kicked a field goal, putting us ahead again.

Now it was up to our defense. All they had to do was stop them from making a field goal. Then Johnny went out there, threw a couple of passes, made a couple of runs, and then ran it in for a touchdown. Game over, we lost.

No way, I thought. *We were on such a good streak. We had this game in our hands, and we lost. The offense didn't do enough to win, and the defense didn't do enough to win.*

I was so upset because I wanted to beat Johnny. That would have been great.

The next game was against Atlanta. We played great against them and won. It was a smooth win, and it meant that we had clinched a playoff spot, even though we still had a few more regular-season games.

The next Tuesday, we came in and had a team meeting. Every-thing was great. We went to lunch, and I had my Apple watch on, and I got an alert from ESPN. It said, *"Alliance of American Football League shutting down due to lack of funding."*

I remember thinking, *Is this real?* I got my phone, opened it up, and saw that it was actually ESPN that was reporting this. I looked up, and I could immediately tell that other people had just seen the same news. We were all kind of looking around like, *Are y'all seeing what I'm seeing?*

We immediately brought it to our head coach, who said, "Hold tight. Let me make some phone calls."

Thirty minutes later, he called an emergency meeting. Sure enough, the guy who was funding the league had pulled out all his money. The league was over.

I remember thinking, *Hopefully, I did enough to get a shot at the NFL.*

We all said our goodbyes, and then we drove back home. I had an apartment, but some players were staying in a hotel, so I gave them a ride. As we pulled up to the hotel, we saw a bunch of stuff out front, and then we realized that it was the team's stuff.

We went inside and talked to the front desk, and they told us, "You guys have been here for over two months, and we have not been paid a single penny. We just found out the league is shutting down due to funding. You guys all have to go today." We were dumb-founded. Some of these guys didn't even have money to go back home because the league was supposed to provide their trans-portation.

As I headed home, I called my agent and asked him, "Do you have anything for me?"

"No, I have nothing," he replied.

"No way," I said. "I'm one of the top quarterbacks in the league. How can I not have anything?"

He called me about a week later and said, "The Eagles want to bring you in for a workout."

I agreed to go, and when I got there, I saw that other AAF quarterbacks were there, too. "I have to crush this workout," I said, and sure enough, I did.

Am I going to get signed? I wondered. *What's going on?* At this point, I didn't know what to expect anymore.

The GM asked me to come to his office, and when I got there, he said, "I'm just going to be honest with you. I had no intention of signing you, but you did so well that I have to sign you."

I remember thinking, *What do you mean you had no intention of signing me? Why'd you bring me in?* It just didn't make sense, but I didn't think anything of it at the time.

I called my wife and said, "The Eagles are signing me." I packed up and headed to Philly.

When I got there, there were only two other quarterbacks: Carson Wentz and Nate Suffeld. I thought, *Oh, I'm good. Teams only carry three quarterbacks. As long as they don't draft anyone, I'm good.* I just prayed that they didn't draft anyone.

This was the beginning of OTAs, so we were doing routes and some light stuff in the weight room, learning the playbook, and having meetings, and everything was great. I was getting along with the other quarterbacks.

The quarterback coach there was Press Taylor, Zac Taylor's brother, and Zac was my quarterback coach when I was with the Rams. There was a relationship there, so I thought, *I'm good. The one thing that can mess this up for me is if they draft the quarterback.*

So, the draft came around, and there was talk that the Eagles were going to draft Easton Stick because he was from North Dakota State. That was where Carson Wentz had been, and they were really good buddies. So, there was some talk that they were going to draft Stick to be with Wentz and have a developmental-type quarterback.

I was in the weight room, lifting, while the draft was on. As I watched, Easton Stick got drafted by the Chargers.

This is great, I thought. *Now I know they're not going to draft a quarterback. This is the guy that everybody was talking about in the draft, and they didn't get him.*

The Eagles had the very next pick, and I thought, *The Chargers already drafted Easton Stick, so I'm good.*

Now, at this point, I already knew how the business worked. When you draft a guy and pay him money, you're not going to cut him, even if the other guy's better than him. I just hoped that I'd get a fair shot.

I went to rookie minicamp, and I crushed it. I mean, I absolutely killed the workout. It was seven on seven. I thought that there was no way I was getting cut.

But after the minicamp, I went online and saw that the Eagles had signed a quarterback from the Browns, a former first-round pick.

Uh-oh, I thought. *I'm the other man now. They're going to call me any second.*

Within an hour, they called me in. "We're going to have to let you go. We just signed a veteran quarterback."

So, again, I got a plastic bag and packed up my things.

I called my agent. "Nothing," he said. "Nothing."

On the bright side beside all that was happening I remember coming home and seeing something on our bed. As I got closer I noticed what it was. It was a pregnancy test. My wife was pregnant! I was ecstatic and was excited for a new chapter as a family.

I said, "Well, I've got to make some money," so I started working for my dad in his bounce house party rental business. I continued to train on the side, trying to figure out what to do next.

My agent calls me about two months later and says, "Detroit wants to bring you in for a workout. You're going to get on a flight first thing tomorrow morning."

I went, and I was the only quarterback there. I had a great work-out, they said, "We really love what you did here at this workout, but right now is not the time to sign a quarterback. You're on our short-list, though."

I went back home and let my agent know what they told me. He said, "Just stay ready because they can call you at any time."

Three weeks later, they called me again. "Why don't you come for another workout?" I went there, but now there were four quarter-backs aside from me. We were *throwing, throwing, throwing,* and I thought, *All right, I'm going to get signed.*

Instead, they said, "We're not going to sign a quarterback yet. We just wanted to see you compared to other quarterbacks."

A month later, they called me again and said, "We're going to bring you back for another workout."

Again, I showed up, and there were other quarterbacks there. I threw the ball and was killing it again. They said, "Go home. We really like you, and we're probably going to sign you, but not right now. Just kind of wait it out. Stay ready."

Sure enough, two weeks later, on my birthday, August 26, 2019, the GM of the Lions called me and said, "We're going to sign you, Perez." He brought me in two days before the fourth preseason game and told me, "We're going to put you on the practice squad. We really love what you did in the workouts. We love your film from the AAF. You're a great developmental guy behind Stafford and all these guys."

I went to practice and was starstruck with Stafford. I was so impressed with his arm, the velocity he put on the football, and how smart he was in the meeting room. He was awesome. He stayed after practice and helped me get ready for the fourth preseason game.

I was just thinking, *He doesn't have to do all of this. What is he doing, helping a young quarterback out? This guy's someone I want to be like.*

He really reminded me of Drew Brees. They were kind of the same type of people.

The fourth preseason game came around, and I was told, "We don't know if we're going to play you or not because you just got here. But regardless, we want to put you on the practice squad."

We were playing the Browns at their stadium. I knew I probably wouldn't get to play, but I was still excited. I thought, *If it happens, it happens. If it doesn't, it doesn't.*

During the game, they threw me in, saying, "You're getting in for a drive. We just want you to get your feet wet." I went out, ran the ball twice, and threw a completion, and then we punted. That was it.

"Great, great job," they said. "You did what you could."

The next day was our day off, so there were no meetings or practice, but I came in anyway and worked out. Afterward, I was sitting next to my locker when I saw a tweet that said, *"Lions trade for rookie quarterback."*

What? I thought. *There is no way this could happen to me again. At this point in my career.* I've become pretty numb to these things, but it still stung.

Sure enough, within the hour, the general manager called me and said, "We just traded for a rookie quarterback. We're going to have to let you go."

At this point, it was just too much. It was an emotional roller-coaster. My position was never secure, and I never knew how long I would be on a team.

I went home and called my agent: "My phone's cold. I have nothing."

At this point, I was thinking, *I'm done. I'm probably going to have to get a real job. But I'm still going to train and stay ready because I don't want to live with regret.* So, I only worked on the weekends with my dad because I had to train all week.

About a month went by without hearing anything, I fell into this dark hole of emotions.

No one was calling me. I saw all my buddies getting workouts left and right, but I didn't get anything. Honestly, I stopped watching football for maybe a month or so.

When Thanksgiving rolled around, I thought, *I'm thankful for the game, the platform it's given me, and the opportunity of just playing in the NFL. I know I haven't done what I wanted, but I touched the NFL field; I'm just thankful.* So, I started kind of getting over this hump of sadness and frustration.

Then I turned on the TV on Thanksgiving, and the Lions were playing.

Okay, I thought. *This is great. I get to see Stafford.* The offense was jogging out there, and when I saw the last name on the back of the jersey, I thought, *There's no way. The quarterback they cut me for is starting right now.*

Sure enough, I looked it up, and Matthew Stafford had fractured his back, so he was out. Then the backup got a concussion, so now the quarterback who would be starting on Thanksgiving was the guy they had cut me for.

I remember thinking, *That could have been me playing on Thanksgiving for the Lions.*

My thoughts began to turn negative. At this point, I really thought, *I'm done. This is it. This is too much to deal with. This is too much stress on my family and too much stress for me.*

And there was no more spring league, either. There was nothing to play in the spring to get more film to get back. So, if you didn't hear anything from the NFL teams, you were done.

Finally, the NFL season was just about over, and the whole time, I just tried to stay positive. My friends and family helped me get over it. They were my support system.

Looking back from my perspective right now, there are a few things I would have done differently from a mindset standpoint.

Back then, it was always my first instinct after a big blow or when something bad had happened to ask, *Why me? Why is this happening to me again?* I would do that for a while before I kind of got over the hump.

Now, my mindset is completely different. If something negative happens, I skip that whole middle step of asking, *Why me?* Instead, I immediately ask, *How do I fix it?* That's a huge game-changer.

In life, you're going to fall down, right? But how quickly do you get up? The longer you stay down, the harder it is to get up. Now, as soon as I fall, I get up. There's no waiting at the bottom. There's no lying down for a long time.

That's one thing that I wish I had known at a younger age because it would have helped me deal with these obstacles and adversity a lot better. There's always a positive in every negative situation. You may not know that positive thing at the moment, but later on, you might realize, *Huh, you know what? This is why I got cut. So I can be in this present moment right now.*

As I've said, a positive always comes from a negative. After so much darkness, I began to see the light, and I got to experience a pretty awesome thing. It was a pretty good deal. I met a guy named Jim Shelly, who had a lot of connections in the football world. He is a big football fan and knows a lot. He saw my story about being a bowler, turning into a quarterback, and learning how to play on YouTube, and he thought that it was a really cool story.

He also had a personal relationship with Kurt Warner, so one day, he called me and said, "Do you want to go to Kurt Warner's house?"

I said, "Um... Absolutely!" He was able to get us connected, and I had the opportunity to go to Warner's house for a couple of days to learn. I got to see how a Hall of Fame mind really thinks.

We watched film and talked about coverages and drops; his training was phenomenal. I wish I could've stayed longer, but that was pretty cool for me, especially since his story was so similar to mine, going from arena football to the NFL, winning the Super Bowl, being named MVP, and then being inducted into the Hall of Fame. That just gave me light and helped me stay positive.

Training at Kurt Warner's house

Soon after that, I saw that there was a new league coming up. *What is this?* I wondered. *A new league? Another opportunity? That would be amazing.*

Sure enough, I looked it up, and it was called the XFL.

EIGHT
XFL AND REDEMPTION

I found out about this league called the XFL. It was originally started in 2001, folded, but was revived in 2020 under new ownership. I called my agent: "What is this XFL thing?"

I did some research on it and discovered some of the rules were unique—different PAT options after a touchdown, double forward passes on a play were allowed, and other things—and perhaps what I noticed most was that in the original XFL, there were hardly any flags. I mean, it looked violent. They wouldn't throw flags for the quarterback, and I remember thinking, *If this is like the original league, shoot, is this what I want to do?*

Then I decided, *It doesn't matter what this league is. I have to play. This is the only thing that will get me to my dream, so I have to do this, whether it's the old XFL or not.*

My agent told me, "It's coming. They're playing in the spring as well. It's just like the AAF. There'll be eight teams, and they're going to have a team in LA. I'll try to get you in LA because it's close to home."

A few months later there was a camp in St. Louis that all the quarterbacks went to. I went, and there were a lot of big-name guys who had started a bunch of games in the NFL.

Again, I was just a guy who had played Division II football and had never really proven himself in the NFL. *I have to outdo these guys*, I thought. *I have to be better than all of them.*

The camp started, and it was business as usual. I felt great. All the teams came up to me and started having more in-depth conversations.

They also mentioned that in the XFL, there were tiers. So, you had tier-one players, tier-two players, and tier-three players, and the salary was based on the tiers. They weren't going to have a draft. The league was going to assign a quarterback to each team. I hoped that I'd be assigned to the LA team because they had a very well-known, established offensive coordinator. He was an offensive guru. Like this is the guy you want to be with.

They were telling me, "You're probably going to be a tier-one guy. We really like what you did. We love your story. We love everything about you. So, keep an eye out for a phone call in a few weeks."

Afterward, I went back home to San Diego and waited. I remember thinking, *I need to influence the league to put me in LA because I don't want to go to a team that's far away.*

I discovered that the offensive coordinator was having a meet and greet in LA. So, I drove there to see him.

"Hey, coach," I said. "My name is Luis Perez. I just went to this XFL showcase, and I really want to play for you. I love your offense. I love what you do. I love what you stand for. I want to play for you."

"All right," he said. "Let's talk."

We chatted for a while and hit it off. Finally, he said, "The league has the final decision, but I really want you in LA."

This is good, I thought. *I did my part.*

Now, when I'd returned from Detroit, my wife and I had found out we would be having a child. So, this whole time, she was pregnant. That's one reason why being in LA and close to family was crucial for us at that point.

A few weeks later, my agent called me.

"Hey," he said, "you're going to be a tier-one guy. I don't know what team you're going to, but I know you're a tier-one guy. They're still figuring out which quarterbacks are going where."

So, I continued *waiting... waiting... waiting... waiting...*

Finally, I got a call from an unknown number, and when I answered, it was the head coach of the LA Wildcats. He said, "I want to meet with you and talk some ball with you. I want to see if you're a fit for what we want to do here."

We met at a coffee shop, he pulled out his laptop, we watched film and discussed it. Right then and there, he told me, "I want you to be my quarterback." I was fired up.

He told the league, "I want Luis." Then he called me and said, "We're going to put you on the Wildcats."

I was thrilled. My wife and I would be close to home, and my family could drive to all the games. This would be great.

Then, a week before camp, the Wildcats signed a veteran quarterback.

I remember thinking, *There's no way they're doing this to me. They just told me I'm a starter.*

Flashbacks from my junior college came to mind. Again, people did not believe in what I was capable of, but I knew how this worked.

I called the head coach and said, "What's going on?"

"The league just assigned us a veteran quarterback," he said, "but I promise you it will be a fair competition. You're just going to have to do better than him."

Keep in mind that the other guy was a 13-year NFL quarterback, while I was just a guy who played a little bit of preseason.

I went to camp thinking I needed to do everything possible to win this job. So, I was the first one there and the last one to leave. I had meetings and walkthroughs with the guys, trying to get everybody on the same page and doing everything in my power to be the guy. The other guy and I were splitting reps 50–50, and we're both doing well.

Then I started noticing my reps going down. Now it was like 70–30. Immediately after that practice, I went to the coach and said, "Hey, you told me this is going to be a fair competition. I'm keeping track of all my stats, and I'm doing really well. What's going on?"

"He has a lot of experience," the coach said. "He's an older guy. We just trust that he's going to be the guy moving forward."

I was devastated. Now, I was going to be a backup in an alternative spring league. No one would sign me if I didn't play. I thought, *I guess I've just got to do better in camp.*

The very next day, the other guy gets hurt. *Oh, yes,* I thought. *This is my time. Like he just got hurt. I feel bad for him, but this is my opportunity to shine. This is it.*

We had two practices where I got all the reps, and I crushed it. Then, the coach called me into his office. I was thinking, *He's probably going to name me a starter.* I just had two of the best practices that I'd ever had.

But when I went to his office, he said, "I don't know how to tell you this, but we just traded you to New York, and you have to leave ASAP."

I was in shock. My wife was pregnant, about to give birth, and now I have to move across the country.

Sure enough, they shipped me off to New York just a week before the first game, and I had to learn a brand-new playbook. They had an established, veteran quarterback who had started games for the Raiders, so now I had to fight just to be on the team.

I flew to New York, and my wife was due at any minute at this point, so I was keeping track of her. Needless to say, I was distraught, thinking, *Why is this happening to me?* As I mentioned earlier, I wish my mindset then had been, *Hey, just move on. Deal with it.*

Two or three days before the first game, my wife said to me, "It's about that time," so I told the coach, "I have to go. My wife's about to give birth."

I didn't want to miss practice, so I took a red-eye flight to San Diego, and I got there at about 8:00 a.m. the next day. My daughter was born, and it was an amazing moment for me—she was born on the day of the Super Bowl, February 2, 2020.

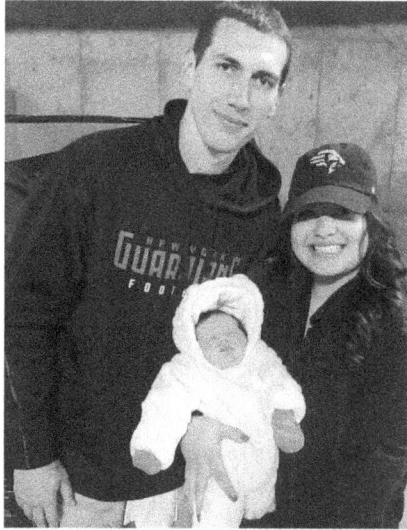

First game my daughter attended in 2020

I was so happy that I could be there for the birth of my first child, and be there for my wife. That was not a moment I was willing to miss. I just felt grateful.

After that, I thought, *This is my motivation. I just need to do more; I have to go back.* I made it back to practice the next day.

For our first game, we were playing the Tampa Bay Vipers, and it was an away game. I was just a board holder at the time, but we won the game. I was happy about that, but I wanted to be playing.

In the next game, we struggled a little bit, and we lost the third game. We were down by a lot at halftime, something like 28–0, and not moving the ball at all. Things were not going well, so the coach made a change at quarterback and put the backup quarterback in. He finished the game, but we still lost.

The next game, they started the backup, and we ended up down by a lot in the fourth quarter. The coach said, "Luis, you're in."

I went in, threw a slant, threw an out route, threw a dig, drive, drive, and then threw a pass for a touchdown. It was the first touchdown we'd scored since the first half. After that, they ran the clock out, and the game was over, but I got that one drive.

That gave me hope that the coach might want to start me next week. I prayed, "If this is meant for me, it's meant for me." At that point, I was ready to move forward, no matter what happened.

The next game was against the LA Wildcats, the team that traded me. I was just hoping that I would start so I could show them what they had lost out on.

The coach brought me into his office and said, "Luis, you're going to be our starting quarterback moving forward. We love what you do."

Again, everything was the same, right? I don't change the way I am. I'll get there early in the morning, leave late, and stay after practice. My motto is to have a strong work ethic. If you do what everybody else does, you'll be like everybody else. You have to be different.

I spent all week prepping. My former teammates with the Wildcats found out that I would be starting, and they messaged me: *"Oh, we're going to kick your butt,"* this and that, talking smack. I just stayed quiet and soaked it all in.

I told my wife, "I really do not care about what anyone has to say. I want to prove to you, myself, my mentors, and everybody who believed in me that I can play." That was my whole mindset.

Pregame, the Wildcats players were all talking smack. I just kind of laughed. I knew how prepared I was, and I knew we were going to beat them. I just knew it.

The game started and I'm playing against Josh Johnson. On the first drive of the game, *boom, boom, boom,* we drove down to the one-yard line, and I threw a fade to score a touchdown. Then they came back: *boom, boom, boom, score.* Then we scored again, and it was 14–7 at halftime.

In the second half, their defensive coordinator changed his whole defense. They were playing certain coverages in the first half, and in the second half, they came out with totally different coverages. So, we kind of struggled a little bit. We were driving the ball, driving the ball, but then we missed a field goal. It was one of those games where we had to fight for every inch. They scored again, and the game was tied at 14–14.

With a minute left, we drove the ball down the field, completion after completion, and got into field goal range. The kicker made it with 30 seconds left. I was so excited. All we had to do was stop them to win the game.

We kicked it off to them, they threw a few incomplete passes, time expired, and the game was over. The New York Guardians won —*we won.*

Playing for the New York Guardians

That was one of the most satisfying moments of my career. Beating the team that didn't want me and let me go was so fulfilling. I didn't really do it for that, but it still felt good. The people who had traded me got to see how they had made a big mistake. That was freaking phenomenal.

The next week, we played the Dallas Renegades, who had Landry Jones and Bob Stoops. Bob Stoops is a Hall of Fame coach for the University of Oklahoma and is a football legend. This was a big game, and we went out there and dominated. It wasn't even close. I threw touchdown pass after touchdown pass, and we won the game.

We were on a roll, 2–0, since I took over as starting QB. I was also the highest-ranked quarterback in the league. Our next game was against the Houston Roughnecks, who were 5–0 at the time, and their quarterback was playing well.

I thought, *If we can dethrone them, this is it.*

All week, I prepped hard, putting in new plays and trying to do everything I could to find weaknesses in their defense. I thought, *This is it. This is the game that's going to put me on the map, beating the undefeated team. We're just going to steamroll past everybody after this.* I felt really good.

We were playing on Saturday, and when Thursday came around, I got on my phone, and everyone was talking about COVID.

"What is this?" I wondered. Then March Madness got shut down, and I thought, *Oh, no, oh, no, please no.*

Sure enough, an hour or two later, we had an emergency team meeting and were told, "The league is shutting down due to COVID. Everybody, go home."

That was so devastating. I didn't even know how to react at that point. I'd been hit by blow after blow after blow after blow. We had all this momentum, and I was the highest-rated quarterback. We were going to play the best team. And now they'd just taken it all away.

I flew back home and called my agent. "Do you have anything for me?" I mean, I was the highest-rated quarterback.

"I have nothing for you," he said. "Right now, the NFL is not signing anybody that's a 'street' free agent because they might have COVID and infect the whole team. So, they're pretty much filtering through guys that are in the NFL right now."

It was such a blow. I didn't know if I could get up from this one. This was a tough one.

I went back home, and everything was closed in California. Everything, even the gyms. I couldn't do anything. I didn't have a gym at home, so I was doing bodyweight stuff. Essentially, we were locked in our house because the whole state was shut down.

I did everything I could to be as prepared as possible. Nobody wanted to run routes. I just tried to stay in tune and stay in shape as best as I could. My brother-in-law became my trainer. He's a former athlete and is very detailed, so he did some deep QB research and helped train me to the best of his ability.

We would start at 5:00 a.m. to run routes and do agility work and some footwork before he had to clock in for work. In the afternoon, we would do the second workout of the day, running hills, plyometrics, and anything to maintain and get better. We trained for months, and I felt great.

That was a key moment for me because I reflected on life, my journey, and everything that I'd gone through to get to that moment. I switched my perspective to one of gratitude and thankfulness for the journey.

I thanked God for all the obstacles he put in my path because that's what molds you. Everything you go through in life molds the type of person you are. And at that moment, I felt really good about where I was mentally, even though the world was shutting down. I was able to find the positive in the negative situation we were in. I just stayed focused and continued to work and work and work and work.

Finally, they started saying, "Now you guys can wear masks and go outside." I got with Todd Durkin and Drew Brees in the summer. I felt like I was back in rhythm physically.

Really, all these moments that happen in life are going to mold you. It's all about the perspective you take.

Perspective is everything because you can always find a positive in every negative. Keeping that positive energy and being able to continue to strive, put your best foot forward, and give your best effort at all times is a great feeling. When I tapped into that, everything changed.

The NFL season started, and my agent said, "You're probably not going to get called because they're not calling anyone from the street."

Since I wasn't going to get any tryouts, I knew I had to find a way to get in front of scouts and throw. Pro days were coming up, and not every school had a quarterback to throw to them, so I had the idea of flying to where I thought the most receivers would be in hopes that they might let me throw.

I bought a ticket to Tampa, Florida, where the best receivers in the country were training for their pro day with the legendary Randy Moss.

I got through the first day, and nobody knew that I was there. I saw that there were not that many quarterbacks but a lot of receivers, so I approached the coach and said, "Do you mind if I hop in?" I told him my resume, and sure enough, he let me throw the ball to these guys.

Everyone asked me, "Where are you from? Where'd you play?" So, I told everyone what my situation was, and then I threw throughout the whole week. I just tried to throw the best that I could in hopes that one of the receivers would ask me to throw to them.

By the end, I felt like I'd had a really good week. Even Randy Moss came up to me and complimented me a lot.

On the last day, I asked the receivers, "Do you guys need a quarterback for your pro day because I'm available? I'm willing to fly to your pro day and throw to you so I can throw for the scouts."

Luckily, several said, "Yeah, we love the way you throw. We would love to have you come." I was ecstatic because I'd taken a leap of faith and just bought a flight ticket with no guarantees that I would end up throwing with any receivers at pro days. We had to go through a process for me to be able to get in, but at the end of the day, we made it happen.

The first pro day I went to was in Buffalo, and it was just me and three receivers. I threw the ball very well, and afterward, quite a few scouts came up to me, so I caught a lot of attention. After that, I went to Western Michigan, where I got more traction. From there, I went to UCLA, and a lot of scouts were there, as it's a big-time school. There was only one receiver there, so I didn't get as many throws.

Now, the biggest one of them all was Louisville. They had five receivers there, and three of them were projected to get drafted on day two, so anywhere between the second and fourth rounds, and that's where I had my best throwing session. I threw probably 150 balls and was on the money. Only two or three passes hit the ground out of all the balls that I threw, and that created a lot of buzz around my name.

I had probably 20 to 25 scouts come up to me, asking me all sorts of questions about who my agent was, where I was from, and what team I played for. That was exciting because they all loved the way I threw the ball.

After that, the scouts said, "You'll be on our list, and we'll keep an eye out for you."

Now, I knew that I had to get some film. Just throwing in a T-shirt and shorts wasn't going to be enough, so I went back home and continued to train.

One day, I was online and came across some news about a new league called The Spring League.

I remember thinking, *What is this?*

NINE
SPRING LEAGUE 2021

Once I heard about The Spring League (TSL), I dove in, trying to figure out what it was. I remember thinking, *I need to play football. Whatever it is, I need to play it.*

My coach from the XFL, Coach Kevin Gilbride, called me and said, "I've been out for a while, and I'm anxious to coach. Do you want to come play in this league?"

"Absolutely," I said. "You're going to coach me?"

"Yeah, if you go, I'll do it."

"All right, let's do it."

So we got in. We were with the Jousters.

I felt an immense sense of gratitude for this new opportunity. Reflecting on my career, I saw God's hand in the timing—new leagues were emerging just when I needed them most. This realization shifted my outlook significantly; I embraced a mindset rooted in gratitude and resolved to focus only on what was within my control.

I had to stay mentally flexible. I had to be ready to adjust and adapt at all times to anything. And I was ready. I had to prove myself once again, not only to myself but to everybody.

The Spring League Jousters (2021)

Every year, I had to grow. You can't just stay stagnant. If you're not getting better, you're getting worse, so you have to constantly be improving at all times.

When I got to camp, I was full of gratitude. They told us, "This is going to be a developmental league. That means everybody on the roster is playing."

That's cool, I thought.

Then the head coach told me, "You're only going to play the first half of every game. The other quarterbacks will play the second half."

This surprised me. Only the first half? That meant I wouldn't be able to lead any game-winning drives. I thought, *This is not it. I didn't sign up for this. This is not what I want to do.* But then again, I switched my perspective to *This is all I have, and I have to be thankful for it.*

My wife was now pregnant with our second at the time, and she continued to support my dreams. She would move to every city I played for, regardless of where it was.

In the first game of the year, we were up at halftime, but we ended up losing. I was devastated. I wanted to come into the game in the second half and win it. I was frustrated, and it was taking a toll on me because I didn't know how to react. I wanted to play the whole game. I didn't want to be on the sidelines for the entire second half. That was killing me.

As much as I talked to myself about staying positive, it was really hard accepting the fact that I had to share time, knowing that I could do much more than I was being allowed to do.

However, throughout that process, I learned that I had more to give the team than just playing well. At the end of the day, all I wanted to do was win. It taught me how to contribute to the team in different ways, like having more receiver meetings, talking to the guys on the sideline, and explaining to them what they should do. I tapped into that, and that's something that I never would have done if my mindset hadn't been right.

I had to be mentally flexible enough to be able to adjust and say, "I'm going to control what I can control. I'm going to play my first half, do the best I can and try to be up in the first half. And the second half, I'll do whatever I can to help the team while not being on the field."

That really taught me a lot. And it was really a cool moment, too, because that was the first time that my daughter was old enough to watch me play. When I went into the game, I wanted her to be happy to see her dad on the field. I wanted her to be proud of her dad, who was playing football, the game he loved, and leaving a legacy behind. It just really taught me what's important in life.

When you have a child, it really changes your perspective on a lot of things. For instance, you become softer and more understanding. You have more empathy and determination to succeed for your kids. It's a feeling that you can only experience if you're a parent. It's one thing to succeed for your family and your wife, but you want to do everything for your kids. You want to provide for them and make sure they have the best lives possible.

It was really a cool time to see how happy she was when she saw me before the game. And then, after the game, she'd run out onto the field, and we'd play catch. Those are moments I will never forget, and I hope that she always remembers them as well.

The season continued, with me playing the first half and the other quarterback playing the second half, and we made it to the championship game. I was fired up about what I would do on the field and then off the field in the second half.

The game started, and I crushed it. By halftime, we were up 17–6. I had thrown two touchdowns and was feeling great. I didn't want to come out because the momentum was just so good. That was probably the best I played all year, and it was the championship game. I was just waiting for the coach to tell me, "Well, it's the championship game, so you can stay in." But he didn't.

The other quarterback went in, and my mindset shifted to *How can I help this team off the field?*

So, I started coaching the receivers, tight ends, and running backs and motivating everybody on the sideline. "Come on! You guys can do it! You guys can do it!"

The other team started coming back on us, and they scored with less than a minute remaining. Now we were down 23–20. I just tried to motivate the guys.

Then I heard the coaches yelling my name: "Luis, Luis, Luis, get in!"

I did not expect that at all. I threw some passes on the sideline, trying to warm up. Then I went back into the game. We had 30 seconds to get a field goal, and I threw a pass here, a pass there, completion, completion. Then I threw a deep pass over the middle, a deep post. The receiver caught the ball and fell to the ground in field goal range. As he was on the ground, the defender, a defensive back, tugged the ball out of his hands, stood, and held the ball in the air, and the ref called an interception. Game over.

Oh, man, that crushed me. I wanted to tell the coach, "If you had let me play the whole game, we'd be champions," but I didn't. I hate losing. I'm a competitor, so I know when I can win games, and losing is just upsetting.

Again, I tried to have a positive mindset, but I couldn't help thinking, *Why is this happening? This is not it. I did not want this.*

The coach from the other team came up to me and said, "Thank God they took you out after the first half. If they hadn't, you guys would have beaten us." Then he kind of smirked at me, and it was just so frustrating.

The season ended, and the first thing I do after every season is call my agent. I asked him, "Do you have anything for me?"

"No," he said. "Nothing, nothing."

The mental toughness you have to have to continue to pursue this dream while getting punched in the face time after time is unbelievable. It's not a good feeling.

I thought that was probably my last shot. I was ready to retire, maybe get into coaching and try something else, because the constant fighting for this dream that was not giving me anything back was very frustrating.

But then I shifted my thought process, telling myself, *Yes, I'm down, but I'm not going to stay down. I'm going to get right back up, and I'm going to push forward and continue to push for my dream. I'm not giving up on my dream.* I didn't know what was going to happen, but I knew that I was going to get there somehow.

The NFL season went by, and I just trained and stayed ready for the next opportunity. Then Drew Brees retired, which meant that I wasn't able to train with him anymore. That sucked.

I started thinking, *Is this a sign to stop?*

Time had passed, and I was still training but hadn't heard much. I started getting in my head once again, and I remember driving one day on my way to the field to throw. I asked God to give me a sign if I should continue or not because all these ups and downs were starting to take a toll. When I got to the field, I opened up my phone and saw that I'd gotten a text from my agent that said, *"Hey, there's a new league coming up again. It's called the USFL. The Spring League is kind of transforming into the USFL. Fox is going to own it."*

When I saw that, I was like, *Wow, God's got me; he's always had.* I said, "All right, I'm back at it. I need to pursue this."

Training at Mt. Carmel High School

Now, when COVID shut down the XFL in 2020, there had been discussions about the XFL coming back in 2022. I'd been in talks with my coach, who was with the Jousters in The Spring League. He said, "I might get a job in the XFL in 2022."

This was great news: two new leagues—the USFL, and the XFL— meant more opportunities. So, I just prepared and stayed ready.

Finally, the USFL was getting ready to have a draft. People were calling me, saying, "Hey, what's going on with you? Are you still trying to play?" There had been some talk that I was done playing.

"I'm still playing," I said. "This is my dream, my passion. I want to continue to play."

So, I basically just trained and waited for the USFL to happen. I was also waiting for the XFL, though, because, again, I didn't know if my coach was going to get the head coaching job there.

I wanted to play for Kevin Gilbride again because I really admired him; he's an awesome coach.

I was kind of in limbo, not knowing if I should wait for the XFL or play in the USFL in 2022. I didn't know what to do. Then Coach Gilbride said, "I just got word that the XFL is getting pushed back to 2023 now. So, the only league in 2022 is going to be the USFL."

So, I called all the USFL teams and said, "I'm not going to play in the XFL." Keep in mind that this is probably a week before the USFL draft. "I want to play in your league. I want to play for you guys."

I asked myself, *Why do I want to play football?"* And the answer came back: *I just love the game. I love what the game brings me. I love the joy it brings to my family. And I want to do it for them. I want to provide for my family.* I'm a big family-oriented guy. I have a small circle, and everything I do is to prove them right.

I had my goals. Everything that was set was short term, but I also had a long-term goal—and I knew that I had to play in the USFL in 2022 to get to my long-term goal. I knew this was my purpose, and I wanted to do this for my family.

I also wanted to continue to grow. I always had this mindset of playing catch-up. I didn't play football in high school, so I had started out far behind everybody else. But I might not be far behind people anymore because I had some experience at this point. That mindset still helped me because it motivated me to keep getting better and better and better.

So, I called all the teams and then waited for the upcoming draft.

KEVIN GILBRIDE – FORMER NFL PLAYER AND COACH

Luis came to us when I was with the New York Guardians. I'm not exactly sure what year that year was, but I think it's when they shut us down as a country. That's when we were playing that spring. So, I think it was 2020.

He was on another team and was not playing, and then he came to us. We had a starter, and we wound up after our third game going to Luis. He was the starter in our fourth and fifth games. He played in that third game a little bit, but we were one and two. And then he became the starter, and we won the next two games.

I would say that the impact that he had on our team was almost immediate. He rallied the team in that third game to where we almost won it when we hadn't been playing very well. And then we won the fourth and fifth games.

After the fourth game, I told the team we were going to vote for captains. We didn't vote for captains immediately. We voted for captains after the fourth game. My intention was to let them get to know each other well enough because nobody had any familiarity with anybody until we came together that December for the first time. And Luis wasn't even there. He was out with the L.A. franchise. So, I wanted everybody to get to know each other.

When we voted, he was almost unanimously chosen as our captain, which was an amazing achievement. That was the respect that the players had for him immediately. So, he turned us around completely.

Certainly, he played better than the previous quarterback as the starter. But a much more profound effect was the impact that he had in terms of changing attitudes and the morale of the team. We were a dispirited team under the previous quarterback who had alienated most of his team.

And now you had a guy who was a charismatic leader that everybody instantly responded to in a very positive, favorable way. And when he asked them to meet extra, to go over strategies that we were employing, watch additional films, or work harder during practice, they responded to his request, his example, in an incredible way.

I mean, I coached professional football for 29 years, and I can honestly say he had as much influence or was able to generate as much influence in that short period of time as anybody I had ever seen.

And I certainly had witnessed a lot of terrific captains and leaders of their teammates. But for him to have done that in such a short period of time, and really in the beginning, not even as the starter but just generating it by the way he handled himself and the way he supported his teammates, it was amazing how he galvanized the approach, the work ethic, the esprit de corps, the confidence, everything. It was just incredible to see.

The next year, we folded because of COVID. They shut us down going into our sixth game, so I was done. I wasn't going to go anymore. And then they asked if I would go to The Spring League, which was the precursor to the USFL, which led to the UFL that exists now.

I said, OK, I would do it. And so I was the head coach of the team, and I can't think of the name of our team back then, but we brought Luis in as a quarterback. And because that was essentially a non-paying league, very few players got paid. Luis was one of them, but not very much. We went to the championship game again, and I think we won 40-something to 40-something.

That led to Fox buying the product because of the excitement of the game. And of course, Luis was the key to it on our side. But because it was non-paying, I played the other quarterback for half the game. I thought that this was kind of a showpiece for a last opportunity to get a shot in the NFL. We were up by two and a half, three scores. When Luis played the first half. In the second half, the other team was able to catch us and beat us at the very end on their last drive.

Had I played Luis the whole game, we would have won easily. He played great. He was a very productive player.

He made our offense very productive. But more than anything else, what always impressed me about him was the way his teammates looked to him for guidance and leadership—and how they responded when he asked them to work a little bit harder or be a little bit more selfless. It was an incredible thing to be part of. I always said what I enjoyed most about professional football was being with the best in the world at what they did. And I witnessed in him one of the greatest examples of leadership that I have ever observed.

I had two years with Luis—one with the XFL and the one with the USFL. But what was amazing is that I recommended him to Jonathan Hayes and Bob Stoops in the UFL, and when he was brought to them, they were like 1-4. And he did the exact same thing with them that he did with us—he helped turn them around and they won the league championship.

So, he certainly is a good football player, an efficient football player at the quarterback position. But it's the intangibles that I think are even more impressive than his football skills.

It's amazing. He is a self-made quarterback, coming from, initially, a professional career as a bowler. And then going to a Division II school and taking them to the national championship. And he won the D-II equivalent of the Heisman Trophy. So, there's some ability there.

The other thing that impressed me was the sacrifices. He's very much a family man. He's always trying to be as close to his wife and children as he can. But to chase his dream, I think it gives you some sense of how important it is to him to make it to the NFL and how willing he is to kind of roll the dice and gamble it all in order to have a chance to accomplish that. It also gives you a feel for the confidence and the competitiveness that he has.

Even though he's been rebuffed two or three times, where he's gone in and thought he made it and then circumstances change at the end, he keeps competing because A, he's a competitor, and B, he has faith and trust in himself that he's eventually going to make it. I think those are pretty strong indicators of the type of guy he is and the competitor that he is.

I can tell you the pain you saw on his face when he had to pull away from his daughter. His first daughter was just born when he was in the

XFL, and it was hard for him to be away. And now he's actually moved his family to Texas so that he can be with them while he continues to chase his dream.

He's an excellent example of a guy who's willing to have faith in himself and belief in himself to roll the dice and see how this thing plays out.

He's done a tremendous job with that. And it goes to show that there's no one path to take to achieve whatever you want to achieve.

TEN
STAYING READY

The week before the USFL draft, I thought, *There's no way I'm not going to get picked. I've been successful in all these spring leagues. There's no way. I've talked to all these coaches and general managers from all these USFL teams, and it seems like there's interest, so I'm ready. I'm ready to take this new step and play in the USFL and prove to everybody once again that I do belong and, most importantly, prove to all the people who believe in me that I can play.*

On draft day, I was sitting on my couch and, with all my family around me, my wife and daughters. It was an exciting time, and we had just had our second child, too. Trying to manage having two babies and job security at the same time, all these different things were happening, and I finally got to the draft, and I thought, *I'm going to get drafted.*

Round one went by. I heard nothing.

Round two went by. I heard nothing.

Round three went by. I heard nothing.

The fourth round went by. I heard nothing.

I remember that moment like it was yesterday: sitting on the

LUIS PEREZ

couch, feeling so disrespected by all these people who made decisions. Not one ounce of me thought about giving up after that.

Instead, I thought, *You don't want to draft me? Well, guess what? I'm going to do whatever I can in my control to be ready for when you call me because I know you're going to call me at some point.* I just had faith that, at some point, somebody was going to call me.

My first instinct was to say, "Well, I'm not going to go to training camp." As a quarterback, you have to learn the playbook. So, then I said, "You know what? I need to find out all these different coaches, and I need to get my hands on all their playbooks."

I reached out to everyone I knew who was on a team and was able to get a hold of every playbook. Then, every day, I studied every playbook, over and over and over again.

The first week of camp went by, and I heard nothing. The second week went by, and I heard nothing. I just kept my head down and studied, studied, studied, trying to do whatever I could to be ready when the call came but also to be there for my newborn.

My wife was juggling a newborn and toddler, all with the uncertainty of what was going on, and what was going to happen. We were also in the process of purchasing our first home in California.

At 27, I was trying to do all these things while staying in shape, staying ready, and studying playbooks. But my mindset was always positive, and I knew—I just had that gut feeling—that at some point, somebody was going to call me.

Week three went by, and still, I heard nothing.

Now we're talking about a week before the first game. I'd been studying relentlessly this whole time, and I was ready. No matter who called me, I was ready.

Finally, I got a call from a coach, and he said, "Our quarterback just broke his toe. Can you come first thing tomorrow morning?"

That coach happened to be the legendary Mike Riley, former long time college and NFL head coach.

"Heck yes," I said. "Absolutely."

124

I got on the first flight the next morning. Keep in mind that we were purchasing our first home, so my wife and family had to pack up and move into our new home without me. It was bittersweet because I should have been there, helping with my daughters and with our move into our beautiful new home together, but I was also pursuing my dream for them.

I had been studying the playbooks for all the teams, so on the first day of practice, I just started spitting out the plays and terminology. The coach stared at me like, "How the heck did you memorize that in one day?" He and I had studied the night before. Needless to say, I did really well in those practices.

The day before the first game of the year, Coach Riley brought me into his office and said, "You've done an amazing job with learning the playbook, learning the system, and galvanizing the team. I want you to be our starter."

I'd gone from being on the couch the week before to starting quarterback. However, I knew I was ready for the moment. I was prepared.

We were playing against the Birmingham Stallions. When we got there, there were probably 30,000 people at the game. It was opening day, and it was on Fox. I mean, it was a big deal.

Coach asked me, "Do you want to kick first, or do you want to get the ball first?"

"I want the ball first," I said.

We got the ball, and in the first game of the year, on the very first play, boom, I threw a 50-yard pass. Two plays later, I threw the first touchdown pass in USFL history. I was so excited.

You couldn't have scripted it any better. I went from being on the couch and studying everybody's playbook to now playing on national TV in front of 30,000 people. I mean, I couldn't have asked for anything better. I just knew that the preparation was going to bring me success. I just knew it.

Now, our other quarterback was a different style of player, and the coach had mentioned to me that there would be some packages for him. So, in the second half of the game, I didn't see the field much, and we ended up losing the game.

I was devastated. I'd thrown two touchdowns in the first half. The ball had barely hit the ground, yet I still hadn't gotten to play much in the second half. It was a very frustrating thing. My first thought was: "Is this going to be like the Spring League? Is this going to be the same thing again?"

We kept playing, but I knew how to handle the situation because I had been able to deal with it in the spring league. It's not that I was okay with it, but I knew how to handle the situation better.

So, the two of us played each game, and we were both doing well. He did his thing, running the ball, and we were passing the ball. We ended up winning nine straight games.

That season taught me so much because I knew how to gather my emotions, change my perspective, apply everything, and I was able to help the other quarterback from the sideline. Now, it still hurt me. I still wanted to play, but we were winning.

In the end, we went 9–1 and clinched a spot in the playoffs. It was an awesome feeling. Keep in mind I considered myself to be successful in every team I've been on.

In junior college, we won a championship. In Division II, we won a championship. In the AAF, we made it to the playoffs before the league shut down.

In the XFL, we made it to the playoffs before COVID.

Now I was in the USFL, and we had a winning record and were going to the playoffs as well.

I finished the season with the best passer rating and highest completion percentage. I was ecstatic, and I was happy with my performance. Now, I didn't put up the numbers I wanted because I was sharing time, but we were winning, and I was very efficient all year. So, I was very excited about that.

For our first game of the playoffs, we were playing a team that we had already played twice in the regular season. Now, it's really hard to beat a team three times. This is because you know each other's schemes and what's going on. It's one of those things where you have to be on your A-game at all times because they know what you're doing, and you know what they're doing. You have to be able to adjust, adapt, and put new stuff in.

The game started, and we were playing well. In the fourth quarter, we were up by three points, and we punted the ball to them. On the punt return, they scored a touchdown with a minute left. Now, we needed a touchdown of our own to win since we were down by four points.

I thought, *This is it. This is my moment. I'm ready to take over and take us to another championship.* So, we drove, drove, drove. On that drive, we had four penalties. I threw a 40-yard pass, and it got brought back. I threw a 20-yard pass, and it got brought back. For one reason or another, we just couldn't get it going.

Finally, the coach dialed up the perfect play. The timing of that play was perfect, and the receiver was wide open. Just as I was throwing the pass, I got blasted, and the ball flew straight up in the air, interception, game over.

Man, oh man, oh man, that hurt. That really, really hurt. We were the favorite to win it all. We were 9–1. For us to lose the way we did was tough. It was tough on my mind. As the QB, it's easy to take the blame. I could have done better.

USFL New Jersey Generals (2022)

I thought that was it for me because, for me to get a shot at the NFL, I thought I had to win it all. And we fell short.

Whenever I go back and watch a game, I'm always thinking, *What else could I have done?* You beat yourself up for it because there are always plays you want back that could have made a difference in the game.

But again, everything you go through in life builds who you are. Everything that had happened to me prior to that point had built me up to where, though I wasn't happy about not winning a championship, my first thought was: *What am I going to do about it?*

The only things that I could control were to train and stay ready. I led the league in completion percentage, and passer rating, and had the best touchdown-to-interception ratio. That was all I could have done. So, I was really happy about that.

Again, my family was super supportive with everything—the whole journey—and I was just really, really persistent. My faith, my family, and my persistence helped me get through all these times. Having a good support system is so important—having mentors, having people who believe in you, who motivate you.

Nothing makes me happier than when I get a video from my wife after the game, and she's with my babies, eating some good food with the game on the TV, watching me play, excited when I score a touchdown. Everybody having fun like that makes me feel so good. It makes me want to continue to play because it satisfies me. It's really cool knowing that my family loves it when I play.

After the season ended, I called my agent and asked him, "What do you have for me?"

"Nothing," he replied. "Nothing at all." At this point, I was just trying to stay positive. I couldn't control teams calling me. All I could do was stay ready and train.

I went home to enjoy my girls and our home for the first time for a bit. You have to realize that I was a year-round player with no off-season because I played in every spring league and was prepared for every NFL season just in case. Downtime was rare for me, so whatever I could get, I enjoyed it to the fullest, especially with my girls.

A week before camp, I didn't think I was going to get signed. Then the Rams called me and said, "We don't even want to work you out. We just want to sign you. We know what you do. You've been here with us before."

All I could think was: *Oh, man. Oh, man. Oh, man. Oh, man.* That day was so fulfilling because I was going back to a team that I thought really liked me. *This is where I'm going to stick,* I said to myself. *They already had me before. They know what I'm about. They know my work ethic, and they love how I operate.*

My wife and I were ecstatic. There was so much joy around the Perez household. It was a surreal moment.

I reported to training camp and was doing really well. I was getting along with Cooper Kupp and Stafford, and they told me, "We kept up with your journey. It's cool to see you continue to play. I'm glad you're back with us." I knew Stafford already because he had been with the Lions when I was with the team, and obviously, I knew Cooper Kupp from when I was with the Rams in 2018.

I loved watching them operate. Cooper Kupp would always be in the quarterback room, he and Stafford were always on the same page. It was such a great atmosphere. They're amazing human beings and amazing football players.

Those two, in my opinion, are the standard of how you should go about your business. It's unheard of for a receiver to sit in on quarterback meetings. Cooper Kupp's drive to become successful was like no other. It reminded me of myself. He had the same obsession for getting better, and Stafford was the same way.

Stafford and Kupp would be there an hour or two before the actual meeting, just the two of them talking about route concepts, how to get in and out of breaks, what they're thinking in this coverage, and how to break off this route versus this coverage and that coverage. I would just listen to their conversations and absorb it all in. It was great.

That taught me so much. It was one thing to be with Drew Brees in the off-season, seeing how he worked with his players, but just as important is the in-season part, watching film, breaking things down, and seeing tendencies in the defense and how to exploit them. It was a constant battle for excellence for them every single day.

Stafford already had a Super Bowl ring from the year before, but he still wanted to be great. That's the standard. It doesn't matter if you're in your first year or your last year. You only go about it one way, and that's going all in. You could tell that those two were all in. They had just won the Super Bowl the year before. The atmosphere around the whole thing was just awesome. The environment was great.

I just sat back for a moment, appreciating the importance of preparation and persistence. Studying all those USFL playbooks allowed me to have the year that I had. Everything in life is connected. It's a game of inches. If I hadn't studied those plays and been ready when they called me, I might not have started the first game. I might not have played all year. I might not have been there with the Rams.

Everything is so delicate. Everything you do, you have to do it with a purpose and with the understanding that it matters to you. Everything you do in life, you have to go all in.

I was having such a good camp. I thought, *I'm good. I'm going to make this team.*

Then, one day during the warmup, I heard a loud pop in my calf, and I thought, *Oh, no. What was that? That hurts. That's pretty bad.*

I didn't want to believe what had just happened to me. I was able to finish practice, but when I woke up the next morning, I could barely walk.

Now, I couldn't go to the trainers and tell them, "I heard a pop in my calf." If they did an MRI and saw something torn, I'd be cut. So, I said, "You know what? I need to go down to San Diego on my day off, drive to San Diego, get an MRI with my doctor, and see what it is."

That's exactly what I did, and sure enough, it was a pretty bad calf strain. The doctor told me that I would be out for about four to six weeks.

"I don't have four to six weeks," I said. "I have practice tomorrow."

I taped it and sleeved it up and took pain medication to try to get through practice, but I couldn't perform the way that I wanted to. I think they noticed that as well, and they told me, "You might play in the preseason, and you might not."

The first game arrived, and I just remember thinking, *If I play, I play. If I don't, I don't.* Everything happens for a reason.

I went to the stadium, and my calf was in excruciating pain. I stood on the sideline, thinking, *Why is this happening to me right now?* Then I quickly refocused and said, "No. I'm going to stay grounded. I'm going to stay positive. All I can control right now is keeping this calf nice and warm. If I get called, I get called."

The game went by, and I didn't get in at all. The next day, they called me in. "Hey, Luis, we're going to have to let you go. We really like what you've done, but right now, there's no room for you. We're going to let the other two quarterbacks battle it out for the two and three spots. You're not going to compete for that anymore."

Here we go again, I said to myself. I had a stronger foundation with my mindset now and was more mentally flexible, able to adjust my mind in different ways. I had been hit so many times, but I just kept getting up, kept getting up, kept getting up.

My first instinct was to say, *Okay, I'm cut. I'll just go home and rehab my calf. Whenever I'm ready, I'll call my agent to get me signed somewhere.* And that's what I did. I went home and rehabbed, rehabbed, rehabbed.

Soon, my calf was much better. I called my agent and asked, "Do you have anything?"

"No, nothing yet," he said.

I enjoyed being home with my daughters, and I spent the year rehabbing, training, and studying the Rams playbook in case they wanted me back. When the GM cut me, he told me, "If we have an injury, we're going to call you." So, I just waited, waited, waited, and finally, Stafford got hurt.

I texted the GM: *"Sorry to hear about Stafford. I'm ready to go. I've been studying your playbook. Let's rock and roll."*

"Hey, Luis," he texted back. *"Hope all is well, but we're actually going to take a look at another quarterback from your previous league and are not going to be signing you at this time."*

That broke me. They told me they were going to bring me back, and then they didn't. That really hurt. That was a tough moment for me. Even with all the positivity that I had around me, that was tough. I had thought it was a done deal, that if someone got hurt, I would get signed. But they didn't sign me.

The year went by, and I didn't get signed anywhere. Toward the end of that season, when I knew I wasn't getting signed, my priorities started changing as far as my perspective on stuff with my family and my faith.

That's the most important thing. If I just keep that foundation of my faith and my family and continue to drive and continue to push my dreams in football, that's all I need.

Staying ready for my next opportunity

So, I just kept that. I continued to be strong in all those aspects, and I got to a really positive place. I had been blessed to play every year because of these new upcoming spring leagues and NFL opportunities, allowing me to take care of my family and do what I absolutely love, which is to play football.

It's easy to get caught up in the frustrating thoughts because stats don't lie, and I know what I'm capable of. I know that I can perform at a high level—I've proven it time after time—but I also understand that some things are out of my control.

I learned this from experience. I fell down and got back up, I don't know how many times. But I was still here, still fighting, still providing, still playing at a high level, and I couldn't always be hard on myself.

I thought, *Now all I can do is play in the XFL again in 2023 because they're coming back.* This time, though, there would be brand-new coaches, brand-new general managers, and different cities. I didn't even know if they were going to want me at this time.

So, once again, I had to prepare and stay ready for the XFL opportunity if it did come.

ELEVEN

CHAMPIONSHIP GLORY AND HEARTBREAK

B eing released by the Rams broke my heart.

Then, all my energy shifted, and I said, "Let's move forward and play in the XFL."

As a part of that process, they had a bunch of different quarterback camps to go to so teams could see what quarterback they wanted. I went to a couple of those workouts and crushed it. I remember thinking, *They're definitely going to pick me this time.*

Before the draft, all the teams do their due diligence on the players and talk to them and all that. So, my agent had talked to a bunch of different teams who were interested in me.

Only two teams called me directly: the Arlington Renegades and the Las Vegas Vipers.

The Vipers called and said, "We really like you. It's going to be up to the league as to where you go, but we really want you."

About a week later, the GM of the Renegades called me and said, "This is Rick Mueller. I want to know your level of interest in playing in our league because we really like you."

I said, "Rick, if you draft me, you're going to win a championship.

I will win you guys a championship." He kind of chuckled a little bit, and I added, "Believe it."

"I believe it," he said. "I believe it."

My agent called me and said, "The league's about to announce where you're going to go." According to him, Vegas and Arlington were bidding for me.

Later, he called me back and told me, "The league wants you to go to the Vegas Vipers. You're going to be their first pick."

I was excited. Vegas was only about five hours from where I lived. The Vipers had a cool name, and their head coach, Rod Woodson, was a Hall of Fame player and Super Bowl Champion. I couldn't have asked for anything better. My mindset at the time was just gratitude and positivity.

Keep in mind that the general manager for the Vegas Vipers had also been the general manager for the LA Wildcats, so when they drafted me, I was a little confused because that was the same general manager who had traded me to the New York Guardians.

Maybe he thought, *I made a mistake before, and Luis is our guy.* That's what I was thinking.

I went to camp, and I crushed it. The team was clicking on all cylinders, and our offense looked really good.

A week before the first game, the head coach called me into his office and said, "We just signed a veteran quarterback."

I immediately thought, *There's no way. He did not just bring somebody in again.* This was the same general manager who had brought in a veteran quarterback a week before camp last time, and now he wanted to bring in another veteran quarterback a week before the first game? I was furious at this point. I mean, I was so upset.

I tried to find a positive in the situation, but all I could think was: *Oh, my gosh. Why is this happening to me?*

We happened to be playing the Arlington Renegades on opening day, the first game of the year and the first game of the XFL season. On the first drive of the game, it was *completion, completion, comple-*

tion, scramble drill, and touchdown. Now I'd thrown the first touchdown pass in two spring leagues, the USFL and the XFL.

First game with the Las Vegas Vipers vs. the Arlington Renegades

For the next two quarters, we dominated the Renegades, and at halftime, it was 14–3. It would have been 17–3, but we had missed a field goal.

However, when we came out in the second half, we started to stall. We had to fight for every inch. The Renegade's defensive coordinator was Tim Lewis. He had been my head coach in Birmingham with the AAF, so he knew my style of play, and he had made some adjustments at halftime.

I wanted to win this game badly because I knew I was on a short leash since they had just brought in a veteran quarterback. The rumor was that they paid these veterans good money, and when you pay somebody good money, you want them to play. That's usually how it goes. So, I knew that I had to do everything I could to earn my job.

In the second half, we ran a screen pass, and I threw in a dumb interception. We were still winning, but I was upset because I knew they were looking for an excuse to take me out.

After that, I returned to *killing it, killing it, killing it,* and we scored another touchdown.

Okay, great. Then we had a play called, and one of our receivers ran the wrong route, I threw the pass where he was supposed to be, and it was picked off. So, now I'd thrown two interceptions in the second half, and the Renegades took the lead.

We got the ball back with less than a minute left. We had to score and go for two to tie the game and go to overtime. So, we drove the ball, *completion, completion, touchdown pass. Boom!*

Now all we had to do was get a two-point conversion to go to overtime. I dropped back, and they sacked me. Game over. We lost.

I remember asking God: *Why? You know how badly I wanted to win this game. You know I'm on a short leash.* I knew that if anything went wrong, they would use it to take me out of the game, so I was devastated. I didn't know what was going to happen in the film room the next day. I didn't know what they were going to tell me.

The next day, sure enough, they told me, "You're going to play next week, but we don't know how much because we're going to play another quarterback."

Oh, my gosh, I thought. *Here we go.*

The next game, I started. As a QB, it's hard to play when you're on pins and needles, thinking that if you make any mistake, you're going to be pulled. That's not the norm. Usually, if a coach trusts you, they ride with you till the end, but I've had the misfortune of always having to be on my toes and play with insecurities.

We were playing the DC Defenders. I went in, and we *drove, drove, drove, drove*—nothing on the ball.

On the next drive, they told the other QB to go in.

After that, I didn't see the field again. They never put me back in. We lost the game.

So, now we're 0–2, and I wasn't playing. By now, I was at my tipping point. I'd been punched and disrespected over and over again. *I don't know how much longer I can take this,* I thought. *I really don't.*

The next game, I only played a few snaps, and we lost again, and now we were 0–3.

For the next game, we were playing DC again, this time in DC. The other QB went in for the first couple of drives, and he hurt his leg. He came out of the game, and I went in.

We were already down 14 points at that time, and it was a rainy game. At that point, I just decided to leave it all out there. Keep in mind that the week of that game, we had just fired our offensive coordinator, so I was basically calling my own plays out there.

I just started driving the ball: *boom, boom, touchdown. Boom, boom, touchdown.* We were *driving, driving, driving,* but they kept scoring, too. *They were scoring. They were scoring. They were scoring.* We had to play catch-up, but we weren't able to, and we ended up losing the game.

I played really well that game, but we still lost. The other QB was still hurt, so this is my shot to take over for the season. I needed to stay focused.

Week five came along, and we were playing the Orlando Guardians (originally my former team, the New York Guardians—the team relocated to Florida in 2023). I felt ready and excited. This was my chance.

As an offense, we just erupted. I was checking plays at the line of scrimmage. I was calling audibles. I was throwing touchdown passes. I threw two touchdowns in the first half and another in the second half. In all, I threw for three hundred yards, and we won the game. That was our first win of the season.

This is cool, I thought. *We're back on track.*

In the next game, we continued to play well as a team. We had a good game plan going in. Now, though, the other quarterback was healthy again, so there was a little more pressure because I knew that if I did anything wrong, I would be coming out. That's no way to play, but unfortunately, in this case, I had no margin for error.

On one drive, we stalled and didn't get anything. The coach said, "If you don't score on this drive, we're taking you out."

Here we go again, I said to myself, *splitting time and playing on eggshells. I deserve more; I know I do. I am capable.*

I went in, and we were driving, driving, driving, but then we got some penalties, and it was third-and-16. I had to score, or I would be taken out. So, I threw a pass, tight window, and was intercepted.

I came out of the game, and the other QB went in. I didn't see the field again that game, and we ended up losing.

At this point, I was just done. I was completely checked out. With all the mental stress that this was causing me and my family, I didn't know if this was what I wanted to keep doing.

After the game, we had the day off, and I decided to use it to watch some film. I went in, and the head coach said to me, "We are going to demote you to number three, so you're not going to be active anymore. We're going to go with the other two quarterbacks."

My jaw dropped. We were already out of the playoffs and had nothing to play for.

He continued, "We're going to try to get some guys some film. You've already had enough film, so you're not going to play anymore."

Now, keep in mind that we didn't get paid unless we were active. We got our signing bonus, but we wouldn't get paid if we were inactive.

I can't do this, I said to myself. *This can't be it.*

I called my wife and flew her out, and we just started talking about what we were going to do with our lives. I contemplated whether I should even play anymore. Every time I was up, I'd get completely shut down—hard.

At this point, I didn't know if I should play football anymore. I had a family, and not having stability had been difficult, especially with two children, not knowing where I would be working next or where we would need to move to. Was this something that we really wanted to do?

Not long after, I was on social media, and I saw that the Arlington renegades had released their quarterback. I thought, *Huh. This is interesting.*

I ended up calling my agent and said, "Can you figure out what's going on over there? They just released their starting quarterback. What's going on?"

He got back to me and said, "I'm going to try to get a trade going to get you over there. They have a quarterback, but he hasn't been doing well."

"That'd be amazing," I said. "I would love that."

I had a couple of buddies who were on the Renegades, and I told them, "Talk to your general manager and tell him that I want to go play for you guys."

My agent was also talking to the general manager of the Renegades, asking, "What can we do?" Soon after, the general manager from the Vipers and the Renegades started talking trade, and I came to find out that Vegas wanted three of the Renegades' starters for me. One guy wasn't even playing.

The Renegades' GM called my agent and said, "We can't do the trade. They want too much for Luis, three starters. We can't do that."

When I heard that, I went to the head coach of the Vipers and told him my situation, that I wasn't getting paid and I needed an opportunity to play so I could have a shot at playing in the NFL.

"I'm not going to do it here," I said. "You guys have made it clear that I'm not going to be active anymore this year, so I'm not going to be able to build my dreams."

In our first team meeting, the coach had said he was all about the players. I said to him, "You talk about being all for the players. This is a good opportunity for you to show that you are and let me go play somewhere else so that I can try to make it back to the NFL."

"Okay," he said, "we're going to work on that."

However, the general manager still didn't want to trade me, so I had to have a heart-to-heart with him.

"Look," I said. "In the XFL 2020, you said I was your guy. Then you brought in a veteran quarterback, paid him a bunch of money, and traded me. Now you're doing the same exact thing to me. You brought me in here. Then you brought in a veteran quarterback and paid him, and now I want to get traded, but you don't want to trade me. I think that's a little unfair."

He told me that he would think about it.

"Please, God," I prayed. "If this is it for me, do it. If it's not, it's not, I'll move on and just figure it out somehow."

Sure enough, the next day, he called me and said, "All right, Luis, we're going to trade you."

Oh, man, I breathed a huge sigh of relief. It was a huge weight off my back. I was traded, said goodbye to all my teammates, and got shipped off to the Renegades.

When I got there, they already had a guy at QB, so I was going in as a backup. I spent the first week learning the playbook. I knew that I wasn't going to be a starter right away, but I also knew that the quarterback they had was struggling, and they were waiting for an opportunity to make a change at that position.

We were playing the Seattle Sea Dragons that week, and as the game progressed, the offense was not doing well, not moving the ball. Toward the end of the game, the QB tore his MCL. I remember thinking, *No way.*

The next day, the coach asked me, "How familiar are you with the playbook?"

"I'm good with it," I said.

So, the other backup, the guy who was originally before me, and I went back and forth in practice to figure out who was going to be the starter for the next game.

After two days of practice, the coach called a meeting and said, "Luis, you're going to be our quarterback moving forward."

Here we go, I thought. Talk about being at the *bottom, bottom, bottom, rock bottom,* and then right back at the top. It's all about how you show up.

The next game, we were playing Orlando. I had already played them earlier in the year with the Vipers, and we had beaten them. I was ready.

The game started, and we played lights out on both offense and defense. We were moving the ball efficiently, driving the ball, *boom, boom, boom, score, touchdown, touchdown.* The defense played great as well, and we won the game.

The next game was against the DC Defenders, who were undefeated at the time. "All right," we said. "This is a great opportunity to dethrone them."

We prepared all week and then went to DC. Keep in mind that I had already played DC earlier in the year and had one of my better games against them as well, so I kind of knew what kind of defense we were going to run and what to expect.

We started out slow and got down early, 26–9. I threw a pick-six earlier in the game due to some miscommunication between the receiver and me. After that, we just methodically *drove, drove, scored, drove, drove, scored, drove, drove, scored.*

Finally, it was fourth-and-15 at our own 25-yard line, and we had to get a field goal to go to overtime. I dropped back and stepped up in the pocket, but the pocket was collapsing. I had a defensive lineman draped over my left side, pulling me down. I threw a 20-yard pass to the receiver, who caught the ball for a first down.

We were still alive. I threw a few more passes, and then I ran the ball out of bounds with two seconds left. Then we kicked a field goal to tie the game, sending it into overtime.

I remember thinking, *All right, this is my chance to dethrone these undefeated DC Defenders.*

Overtime was like a penalty shootout. Each team got one chance from the five-yard line, and the best out of five would win.

On the first one, we got it. Then they got it.

Then we missed it, and they missed it.

Then they went first, and they got it, so we had to make it to keep going.

The coach called the perfect play. I mean, it was a great play call. The guy was wide open. I threw the ball, and a defensive lineman jumped up and barely tipped the pass, incomplete. Game over, we lost. That sucked.

We had one more regular-season game. We were playing against the Houston Roughnecks next, but another team had to lose for us to have a chance at the playoffs.

I remember thinking, *This is crazy. Our fate depends on another team's loss.*

Thankfully, the other team ended up losing, so we made the playoffs. That meant that this game against the Houston Roughnecks was kind of meaningless. The team that needed to lose had played just before us, so we knew going into the game that we were in the playoffs. We also knew that the Houston Roughnecks would be our first opponents when the playoffs started, so we didn't want to show them too much or for any of our guys to get hurt. Because of that, we didn't use any of our best plays, and we ended up losing that game.

After that game, we went back to the hotel, and I talked to God, telling Him how grateful I was. I thought back to the first game of the year when the Vegas Vipers had lost to the Arlington Renegades, and I'd asked God, "Why did I lose this game?"

Now I realized that If the Renegades hadn't beaten the Vipers in week one, they wouldn't have been in the playoffs.

God knew what He was doing, and it was a reminder to always have faith. There's always a bigger plan in place that you may not know about. Just do your part, stay positive, keep your head down, and continue to grind. That's it.

The next week, we were playing against the Roughnecks again, and they were a really good team. We were the underdogs, especially since they had just beaten us. We were just happy to be in the playoffs, but we knew we were a good team because we were saving all of our good plays.

So, we went out there and played with house money. We had nothing to lose. I told my teammates, "Everyone is counting us out, but only we know how much work we put in. We know what we can do. If every single one of us does our job to the best of our abilities, we will dominate."

Our first drive of the game was probably one of the best drives that we had all year: completion, completion, long run, completion, long run, completion, boom, scramble, drill, touchdown pass, 7–0.

Our defense got a three-and-out, and then our offense was up again: drive, drive, drive, score, 14–0. The defense got another stop, and then it was drive, drive, drive, field goal, and we were up 17–3.

We were stunning everyone.

Coming out in the second half, Coach dialed up the perfect play —one we had been practicing all week for this specific coverage. Sure enough, on third-and-seven, we got the look we wanted, and 50 yards later—touchdown!

Then they tried catching up a bit, but it was too little, too late. We won the game, we won the South Championship, and we were going to the championship game.

We were all ecstatic. I went from being on the bench to now playing in a championship game. It was a surreal moment.

I remember thinking about how hard work pays off and how my

faith kept me grounded. All these different things had to happen perfectly for me to be in the position I was in. To say that I felt blessed at that moment would have been an understatement.

In the championship game, we were playing against the DC Defenders, the team that beat us in overtime during the regular season. We were excited to get back at them because we didn't like how that had gone down.

I studied my butt off all week, and I was as prepared as I've ever been. The game was in San Antonio, and when it started, I was on fire. We just *drove, drove, drove, touchdown, drove, drove, drove, touchdown*—pass after pass.

I was checking plays at the line of scrimmage. I was giving audibles. I was doing so many different things. And when I looked up at the score at halftime, it was 17–6 in the championship game.

Right before that, I'd gotten sacked. The defensive lineman had landed on me kind of funny, and I had heard a pretty loud pop in my foot, but I didn't think anything of it at the time. Adrenaline was pumping. But during halftime, it felt hot and started hurting, and I thought, *This is not normal.* I was too focused on winning, and like I said, adrenaline was pumping, so I took some ibuprofen and continued to play the game.

We kept dominating. We were like nine for nine on third down. I mean, it was just complete domination.

Late in the third quarter, it was third-and-15. We had to get a first down to keep the drive going. I called a quarterback draw, which they would never expect, and got about 20 yards and the first down. The crowd erupted, and the sideline erupted. We were excited.

We *drove, drove, scored.* The game was getting out of hand. We ended up scoring 35 points. The DC Defenders could never catch up, and we ended up winning the championship 35–26.

I just remember that feeling of gratitude when I took that last knee. The power of persistence, the power of faith, the power of a strong support system, all these different things had to happen this way for me to be there at that moment. Then, the cameras rushed to me right after the game, and I started interviewing.

"Hey, how does it feel to get traded halfway through the season? You know, a lot of people would have given up and just stopped. What motivates you to keep going?"

Then the interviewer asked me, "How sweet is this moment?"

I said, "Everything you go through in life, all the obstacles, all the adversity, all that makes the moment special. If it were easy, everybody would be good every year, right? It's not as satisfying as going through all those obstacles. You know, giving up is not in my playbook. That's not what I do. I have a dream. I have a passion. I have a desire and an obsession like no other. And I want to go to the NFL."

Once I finished my interviews, my family rushed down, and we hugged and cried. There was confetti everywhere, and we were making angels in the confetti. Both my daughters were having a blast. Everyone had happy tears. Old coaches were there, and old childhood friends had flown in, as well as old teammates. It was just a surreal feeling.

After that, there was a ceremony on the field where they awarded us the championship trophy and were going to announce the game's MVP. Dwayne "The Rock" Johnson was there, and he was congratulating Bob Stoops and the Renegades for winning the championship. It was just such a good time.

I knew I was going to be in the running for MVP. I had played a really good game, but I didn't know for sure if I would get it. I just remember The Rock saying, "This quarterback got traded. How about this season? With three touchdown passes and three hundred yards... your Championship Game MVP is Luis Perez."

Receiving the MVP award after the Championship Game with Arlington (with UFL co-founders Danny Garcia and Dwayne "The Rock" Johnson)

He gave me a hug, and I patted him on the back. Then he handed me that trophy. It was a feeling like no other.

I told him, "Thank you so much for creating this league. I really don't know where I'd be in life right now if it weren't for you guys pursuing spring football and creating this platform for players."

I hugged it out with him and then just sat back and reflected on everything that had happened. My whole body felt numb. We went back to the locker room, and we all celebrated. There was champagne everywhere, cigars everywhere. It was a great time.

I saw my general manager there, and I went up to him and said, "Remember what I told you when we had the phone call before the season? I told you I would do it. I told you I'd win you a championship." That was a memorable moment.

Unfortunately, my foot started acting up, and I had to attend to it. I saw our doctor, and he said, "Your foot's really swollen. It's so swollen that we can't take an x-ray. So, tomorrow morning, can you come to the office and get an x-ray so we can check you out?"

"Sure," I said.

That night, I celebrated with my family, enjoying the moment, but the pain in my foot was getting worse and worse. *Oh, man, I thought. I just hope this is not too bad.*

I talked to my agent, and he said, "This is awesome. You've got a lot of NFL interest. What you just did was amazing, pushing that team around halfway through the season and taking them to a championship. This is going to be your shot to get back to the NFL."

The next morning, I went to the doctor's office and got an x-ray. I still remember the distraught look on the doctor's face when he walked in. "Your foot's broken," he said. "You're going to be out for probably eight to 12 weeks."

My heart sank. After everything that I had gone through, my shot at getting back to the NFL had just gone out the door.

Feeling numb, I called my agent and told him, "I broke my foot."

"What?!" he said.

"Yeah, I broke my foot." I didn't tell anybody else but my wife that my foot was broken.

That whole season was just so bittersweet: winning a championship, knowing that I was going to get all these NFL opportunities, and now having nothing because I had to rehab a broken foot. That took a toll on my mind.

At the time, I didn't know if that was it. I wondered if it were a sign telling me, "You've been pursuing this too long. It's time to move on and do some other stuff." I didn't know what to think.

After a while, I just remember getting over the hump and feeling gratitude for everything, and understanding how I had no control over that. I got back into a positive mindset and returned to grind mode, thinking, *I have to rehab and get ready for the season.*

So, I rehabbed my butt off. I mean, I was rehabbing, rehabbing, rehabbing. But my foot was taking a long time to heal, and I was not recovering as quickly as I would have liked. I remember thinking,

Everything happens for a reason, and I took time to grow mentally, physically, and spiritually.

Again, it's all about having gratitude and changing your perspective on things. There's always a positive in every negative. If you change your perspective to a positive one, your life will be so much better.

Doing that gave me even more confidence than I'd had before. I had kind of lost my confidence when they'd wanted to bench me with the Vegas Vipers. But with the Renegades, I played for coaches who really believed in me. I hadn't had that feeling since Commerce, when I was in college and won a championship. When coaches truly believe in you, that's when you strive. Having a coach who believes in you is so important because it enhances everything.

I knew this was just another stepping stone to get to my goal. I knew I just had to overcome it. At this point, I'd gone through so much that this was easy. I just had to get over this rehab and get right back in it. Throughout the whole process, it was all about having faith, staying grounded, and relying on my support system.

Again, you don't know where God's going to take you. You don't know the detours. You may not know at the moment why God does certain things, but at some point, you might find out, just like I did with the first game of the year, when I was with the Vipers and we lost to the Renegades.

At the time, I asked God, "Why are you doing this? Why is this happening to me?" Well, it turned out that the Renegades needed that win against the Vipers to get into the playoffs and for me to be able to win a championship.

So, you have to stay grounded and faithful. Control what you can control. Continue to work hard and be persistent in everything you do. That molds you into a resilient human being. That's ultimately what you want in life. No matter what comes your way, you should be able to adjust, adapt, move forward, and address it. That's all you want to do.

So, I rehabbed throughout the whole process. I knew my shot at playing in the NFL that year was done. I remember thinking, *Okay, I'm going to go back one more year. If I have a full year with the Renegades, I know I'm going to get a shot at the NFL again.*

I rehabbed and studied playbooks during the off-season, and I watched film every day. I was relentless in my pursuit of being great. I missed out on family parties on the weekend because I had to do things like participate in seven-on-sevens. I didn't care about anything else except providing for my family and succeeding for my wife and my daughters and everybody else who had been there with me through it all—and I mean all.

I knew that this was going to be it. I was getting older, and I really wanted to make it back to the NFL before it was too late. So, this was the strongest off-season of my career.

This was it. It was time to go back to what was now the United Football League (UFL) for one more year.

CHUCK LONG – ARLINGTON RENEGADES OFFENSIVE COORDINATOR AND FORMER NFL QB

I was coaching with the Renegades, the Arlington Renegades, in the XFL, and we had a set of quarterbacks. We had three quarterbacks, and we were going through the season, and two of our quarterbacks essentially got hurt. Our starter got hurt, and we had to go find a quarterback. So, we traded for Luis when he was with the Las Vegas Vipers.

Ironically, we played against Luis in the very first game of that year when he was with Las Vegas. And then there we are, I believe it was week six, and we had to trade for him because we needed another quarterback. So, that's how the relationship started.

I've been coaching for over 20 years now, close to 25 years, and I've been a quarterback coach to some degree for most of those years, My point is I've coached a lot of quarterbacks. There are two guys of all the quarterbacks that I've coached over 25 years or so that stand out as far as all those attributes, the knowledge of the football game, leadership qualities, work ethic, all those intangibles that make people great in any business, in any walk of life. They just knew the offense in and out.

The first one was in college when I was at the University of Oklahoma and coached Josh Heupel. You'll have to google Josh Heupel. He's now the current head coach of the University of Tennessee. And they did well this year (2024). They got into the playoffs. So, that's the first one.

The second is Luis Perez. Luis is unique and different from Josh because Josh Heupel grew up with a coach. His father was a longtime small college head coach, so he grew up with it, whereas Luis Perez did not.

Luis had to learn how to play quarterback from YouTube videos—I'm sure you're aware of that. And he didn't even play high school football. So, it's just truly amazing where he is today with his knowledge of the game.

I have so much trust in Luis that when we put a game plan together, he's right there doing most of it. I always want my quarterback to be comfortable in the system, but he is so intelligent and has such a good feel for the game that I let him do most of the planning.

It's amazing what he's learned just by watching videos, but there's a lot out there now. He's self-taught. Some people go to piano lessons and guitar lessons, and then some are just self-taught musicians. They don't need a teacher.

Luis is definitely your self-taught man. It's one thing to teach yourself and then to just be a good football player, and then it's another thing to go pro. Yeah, going pro is hard, and it's hard to stay in pro football. It's one thing to make it, but it's quite another to stick to it. And he's done both. He has dreams of the NFL, and hopefully, that'll happen. Never say never. But right now, he's become the "King of Spring." That's what they're calling Luis right now. Yeah, he's the "King of Spring"—King of spring football.

The thing about Luis is, as I mentioned, how he masters the game and masters the game plan, and knows the game of football. As for his leadership and his toughness? The best story I can tell you is that we were a losing football team three years ago. Not only did we lose our starting quarterback, but we didn't have a great record. We were fighting to get into the playoffs. It was a fractured football team. We were not in sync. We didn't have really good chemistry on the team.

When we got Luis, that changed overnight. He galvanized our football team. He brought everybody together for a common goal. It was really unique to just see that right before our eyes. Immediately, they gravitated to him. You always want a quarterback that your teammates gravitate to, and they immediately gravitated to him.

He got us into the playoffs—not only got us into the playoffs, but we won the championship. We won it all, and a big, huge part of that was his leadership and the way he positively galvanized our football team. I hadn't seen anything like it because we were going down fast, and he came in, and the whole thing turned around.

He's been a joy to work with. Again, he thinks about his teammates first all the time. As we're game-planning, he does a great job of that. I think that if he wants to, he'd be a great future head football coach. Obviously, that's his choice whether he wants to get into coaching or not, but I know he'd be a really good one.

TWELVE
SCALING TO THE TOP

That offseason, I was obsessed with going out there and being the best quarterback I could be and the best version of myself on the field. I wanted to do it for my family, the coaches who believed in me, and my kids. This obsession was like no other. It just kept building every year, and I got bigger, faster, and stronger.

I was excited to go to camp and show all these people all the work I had put in. I got there and had the best camp of my life. Not a single ball hit the ground. It reminded me of my college days and how dominant I had been. I give credit to my coaches for this because they gave me the confidence I had in college.

This was also the first time since college that I was able to come back to the same system again. Every year, I had been forced to learn a new system. That was huge for me, especially considering the type of player I am. I knew the plays like the back of my hand, and I was playing with confidence.

The XFL and the USFL had merged to become the UFL (United Football League). They had taken the top four teams from each league and put them in one league, so there were eight teams total.

This meant that the competition would be better, and I knew that going in

On opening day, the first game of the year, we were playing against the Birmingham Stallions, who had won the championship in the USFL. So, it was the XFL champs against the USFL champs.

I thought, *The Stallions are a great football team, so this is my chance to just play all out and do well.*

The game started, and I threw the first touchdown pass of the season—which also made it the first touchdown pass in the UFL. I can officially say that, and that's a pretty good feeling.

As the game went on, we battled back and forth. We'd be winning, and then they'd come back. We would take the lead again, and then they'd come back again.

Late in the game, we just couldn't get an inch. I threw a bad interception, and they ran out the clock, and we lost.

Man, I thought, *here we go.* I cannot stand losing. This was a chance to prove to everybody that I can play at a high level. I played a good game, but it wasn't my best game. Their defense coordinator had done a good job, but it was still frustrating.

So, we started 0–1. This was not how we wanted to start, but it was okay because we could redeem ourselves.

In week two, we went to St. Louis, and it was opening day for them. They had 50,000 people at their first home game—it was unreal.

We were up against A.J. McCarron, a top quarterback who played seven seasons in the NFL, and we duked it out, back and forth, *boom, touchdown, touchdown, touchdown, touchdown, touchdown.* At halftime, we were tied.

In the second half, we came out strong—*they score, we score.* Finally, the fourth quarter came around, and we were driving the ball. It was still a tied game, 24–24. There was probably a minute left, and we were almost in field goal range. It was third down, and we didn't convert. At this point, there were about 30 seconds left.

Our kicker came out onto the field and missed the field goal. They got the ball back and threw a long pass. They did a running back draw for a big gain, plus there was a flag on defense. Just like that, they were in field goal range. As time expired, they kicked a field goal, and we lost.

Now we were 0–2. We'd gone from defending champs to the bottom of the division. This was not what we had expected. We were a good football team. I was crushed. Like I said, I cannot stand losing. You can always take lessons from losing, but it still feels bad.

Now, I was playing well. I was having individual success, but we were not winning, so I couldn't enjoy my success. At this point, I was leading the league in passing yards and touchdowns.

Week three came around, and we were playing the DC Defenders. We had just beaten them last year in the XFL Championship game, so we knew that they had us circled on the calendar and would give us their best game.

The game started, and we were dominating. It wasn't even close: score, drive, drive, score, drive, drive, score. Our defense was making stops, too. With only 50 seconds left, we were up 24–14. Then we kicked a field goal to make it 27–14. On that drive, a defender fell into my knee, and something about the joint felt off.

We kicked the ball to them, and they returned it all the way to the 50-yard line. Then they threw a couple of passes and scored.

There were now about 20 seconds left, and the score was 27–22 because they went for two and made the conversion. Next, they went for it on their own 25-yard line to try to get the onside kick—and they got it. Then they drove, drove, drove, and scored a touchdown.

The game ended as time expired, and we lost 28–29.

I thought, *Whoa, this is not what I signed up for.*

I knew something was up with my knee. I had torn my MCL in college, so I knew that I had injured it again, but I didn't know how bad it was. I'd put a brace on and had been able to finish the game.

I thought it would be fine, but when I woke up the next morning, my leg was so swollen that I couldn't move it. I thought, *There's no way. We're 0–3, and I can't move my knee.*

Again, you try so hard to find a positive in every negative situation, but that's hard to do. It's not realistic to do it every single time. Naturally, the human response is to say, "This sucks." I had no idea what I was going to do. I didn't know how bad it was or anything.

I went to practice, taped it up, and put a brace on it. *Okay,* I thought, *I might be able to play.* In my mind, I knew I was playing no matter what, but I wanted to convince the coaches to play me, so I was doing everything I could to make sure of that.

The fourth game of the series came around, but when it started, I quickly realized that I could not move. I couldn't move out of the pocket or step into my throws. I didn't play well at all, and we lost the game.

Now we were 0–4. Statistically, I was still leading the league, but I could not enjoy it because the team was losing. However, after that game, I started to feel more optimistic. *I can do this,* I said to myself. *It doesn't matter if I'm going through this injury. I will find a way to get it done. It does not matter.*

Around that time, the locker room was starting to divide because we were losing. People were starting to get frustrated and upset. They wanted to do more, but in reality, we just had to keep doing our jobs. We should have been winning all these games; we just needed to believe and finish strong. We needed to stay the course, focus on ourselves, and keep getting better.

The next week, we were playing San Antonio, and they were a good football team. My knee was also starting to feel a bit better, and I was a little more mobile.

The game started, and we were playing good football—we just missed too many opportunities. On one play, when I threw to a wide-open receiver, he lost the ball in the lights, and it went right over his head. He didn't even see it.

On another play, we called a double move in the red zone, and I overthrew him. It was fourth-and-1 on the opposing team's 20-yard line. Instead of kicking a field goal, we went for it and got stuffed. Then, when we tried to kick a field goal, they blocked it and almost returned it for a conversion.

That was the type of game we had that day. Nothing clicked. Despite all that, we still had a chance at the very end, but it was too little, too late, and we ended up losing by just a few points.

Now we were 0–5, and I didn't know what to think at this point. Again, I was having a lot of individual success, like leading the league in passing touchdowns, but it was wild to go from champs to one of the worst teams in the league.

I wasn't throwing any interceptions, and I had the most yards and the highest completion percentage, but these things did not result in wins.

I started to ask myself, *Can I do more? Should I try to press and do more?*

Coach Long told me, "No, you're playing great. Just continue to do what you're doing. We're going to get our defense going. Our offense is going to get going. Our special teams are going to get fixed. Just keep doing what you're doing. Don't press. Don't force it. Just keep playing how you're playing." That was great advice. I had to believe in myself and stay the course. We just had to keep getting better and better.

Our next game was in Michigan, and we were playing in a dome with a great atmosphere. My knee felt a lot better at this point. We played well, and we dominated this game.

On offense, it was *boom, boom, score, boom, boom, score.* Our defense was stopping them, too. We were just rolling. We looked like we had in camp, and we felt really good.

The fourth quarter came around, and they scored two touch-downs late to take the lead by two. Now we had to drive and get in field goal range.

We started with the ball at our own 25-yard line and drove the ball—*completion, completion, completion, completion.* Now we were in field goal range. They had no more timeouts. We had a great kicker.

We thought, *This is our game. This is going to be our first win of the season.* All we had to do was run the ball a few times just to kill some extra clock so we could kick the field goal and win by one.

On the next play, we handed the ball off, and our running back got hit. He fumbled, but we recovered the ball. He was hurt, though, so we had to use one of our timeouts, which stopped the clock for the other team.

On the play, we lost four yards. I thought, *I'm going to try to get them to jump offsides to try to get those yards back and make it easier for the kicker to make the field goal.*

I went through the cadence, got them to jump, and threw a 50–50 ball, thinking that it would be a free play. Well, guess what? They didn't throw a flag. So, now we stopped the clock for them again, and it was third-and-14.

We decided to run the ball and eat up some more clock. We handed off, and the running back got one or two yards. At this point, there were still about 20 seconds left—we weren't able to run the whole clock out.

We kicked the field goal, and it was good. Our sideline erupted. All we had to do was contain them on the kickoff.

On the kickoff, they returned it all the way to the 50-yard line with ten seconds left. Unfortunately, one of our defenders grabbed the returner's face mask, so they got another 15 yards.

Now they were at their 35-yard line, which is field goal range, and they had the best kicker in the league, a guy who currently plays for the Lions. We thought, *It's over. We just blew it.*

The kicker went out and missed the field goal. Again, our side erupts with excitement. We all thought that we'd finally gotten our first win.

Then we saw that the ref had thrown a flag.

We'd had 12 men on defense, which meant a five-yard penalty and re-kick.

They moved up five yards, and he got another chance at the field goal. This time, he made it, and we lost, so now we were 0–6. Again, I had a lot of personal success in that game—no turnovers, two or three touchdowns—but it didn't matter.

In the locker room, helmets were thrown, and holes were punched in the wall; everybody was extremely upset. The coach gathered us together and said, "We have to be more detailed, guys. We have to be more detailed in everything that we do. You have to be more intentional."

Our next game was against Memphis. "Let's just play loose," we said. "That's all we can do. Let's go out there and have some fun."

We went out and scored 47 points, the most anyone in the league had scored all year. Our defense played great, too. We dominated and beat them by 30 points. I threw three touchdowns, efficient again.

Finally, we'd gotten our first win. We were fired up, and we said, "Let's carry this momentum into the next game."

The next week, we were playing St. Louis again. In the first game, remember, we'd only lost to them by a field goal and should have won. So, we had something for these guys.

We absolutely dominated that game: *drive, drive, score, drive, drive, score, drive, drive, score, drive, drive, score.* In the end, we beat them 40–20. We killed them.

Now, we were really excited—we were on a roll.

Our next game was against San Antonio, a good team with one of the better records in the league. The game started, and we were fighting for every inch. There were some mishaps early in the game, and we missed some opportunities. Both teams scored back and forth.

It was a really close game, but we ended up losing by three

points. Again, I had a good game, but it didn't translate into a win. That loss killed all of our momentum.

It was time for the last game of the year, and we were playing against the DC team again. They'd barely beaten us earlier in the year. "We have to win this game," we said. "We have to finish strong. We know we're not making the playoffs anymore, but we can finish strong."

For most of the game, we just dominated them—*touchdown, stop, touchdown, stop*. Then, late in the game, they started creeping back. I threw an interception on a 50–50 ball, only the third interception I had thrown all year, and I was pissed with myself for that.

Then, they scored and took the lead. After dominating them all game, we were now down and would need to score a touchdown to win. We were backed up to our own 20-yard line, and we only had about 50 seconds to score.

The coach called some great plays, and we drove all the way down to the red zone. It was third and goal, and we were at the ten-yard line. I stepped up in the pocket, moved left, and threw a pass to the back of the end zone: touchdown. The defense got a stop with about ten seconds left, and we won the game.

That season, I led the league in touchdown passes, passing yards, touchdown-interception ratio, and completion percentage. We had the second-best offense in the league. We were number one on third-down conversions and had the fewest turnovers.

Despite all that, we lost more games than we won, and we didn't go to the playoffs.

Unfortunately, NFL teams don't want somebody who doesn't win. They want winners. So, it was a bittersweet moment. Yeah, I lit all the stats up, but we didn't even go to the playoffs.

The season was over, and I said bye to everybody: "Hey, I love you guys. Let's reflect and stay in touch throughout the off-season." Then I wondered, *Well, what's next?*

I called my agent, and he said, "I've got nothing for you, man. I have nothing. You guys didn't have a great year."

I'd already heard this story, so as the summer went by, I continued to train and stay ready. I also enjoyed the time I had with my kids and wife.

Finally, training camp came around, and I thought, *All right, I should get a call any minute.* But after a week, I still haven't heard anything. I was devastated because everybody was full, and now I had to wait for an injury to get picked up.

In the second week or third week of camp, I got a call from the Chargers, and they said, "We want to bring you in for our workout."

"Yes," I said, thinking this was my opportunity. I grew up in San Diego, a Chargers fan, and I'd watched Drew Brees play in Qualcomm Stadium. The first game I ever went to was a Chargers game. I'm a diehard Chargers fan.

I remember going to games and saying, "One day, I'm going to put on that jersey." I even told my family that over and over.

You lose sight of that. Once you're in the mix in the NFL, you lose sight of those moments. But when the Chargers called me, I remembered telling myself as a kid, *I'm going to put on a Chargers jersey, and I'm going to play for them.* That dream was about to become reality.

I went to the workout, and I was the only quarterback there. I threw some passes, boom, boom, boom, and was doing well. Very few balls, maybe one or two, hit the ground. Overall, it was another great workout.

Afterward, they said, "Go to the lobby and just hang out there. We'll talk to you in a bit."

As I sat there, waiting, everybody was texting me: *"How'd it go? How'd it go? How'd it go?"* I remember thinking, *I killed it, but I don't know what's going to happen.*

Finally, they came out and said, "We're going to take you to do a physical."

I really hope I pass, I said to myself. I'd just hurt my MCL and was still kind of recovering.

I did the physical, and they said, "You passed. We're going to sign you."

Talk about a full-circle moment. I couldn't believe that I would actually be wearing a Chargers jersey. I had to take a moment and process what had just happened.

This was very special for me and my family. It just showed me how faith and focus are so important, as is creating a plan and sticking with it. Trust the process, and you'll reach your goals. I did, and now I would be with the Chargers. I was excited and ready to go.

I got there, and for the first couple of days of practice, I crushed it. Greg Roman, the offensive coordinator, and Jim Harbaugh, the head coach, both spoke highly of me in press conferences, and I thought, *Oh, my God, this is good.*

Playing with the Chargers and Head Coach Jim Harbaugh

In the first preseason game, I went in in the fourth quarter and did my thing—threw some good balls and completed some passes. Afterward, they said, "You did a great job. We like what you're doing, and we're going to keep you around. We're going to release these other two quarterbacks."

Now, there were only three quarterbacks: Justin Herbert, Easton Stick, and me. *This is phenomenal,* I thought. *This is awesome.*

In the second game, I went out there and played a little bit more, and I did well again. I wished I were a little more mobile; I knew what I was capable of, but I didn't have much time to showcase myself, and I did not want to make any mistakes. I was excited for the opportunity to be on the practice squad, and I was fired up.

I was never really competing for the second spot. I was only competing for the third spot. So, in the third game, they let the backup play the entire fourth quarter. We ended up winning the game, and they said, "We're going to put you on the practice squad."

I was thrilled. I was from San Diego and had grown up a Chargers fan, and all of my buddies were Chargers fans, too. Now I was playing for the team. You couldn't have scripted it any better.

They told me that I would be on the squad all year. Then they said, "Go get your stuff, and then come back in the morning and sign your paperwork."

I drove down to San Diego and told everyone that I had made the practice squad. I was on cloud nine. This was my moment.

Then, early the next morning, I drove back up, and everybody was there, signing their pre-squad paperwork. Finally, they called me into the office, and I was ready to sign.

Then they said, "Luis, we have some bad news. We just traded for a veteran backup quarterback, so we're going to put Easton Stick at number three, and we're going to bump you out."

That destroyed me. That was the toughest cut I'd ever had, especially after everything I had gone through in life—all the hard work, the persistence, the faith, keeping the dream alive, and all the sacrifices. But I just thought, *Well, I can't do anything about it, so what's next?*

I went home, and my family was so disappointed—not in me, but in the situation. I knew that they felt the same way I did and it was not easy on anyone. I cheered them up, saying, "Hey, it's all good. We're okay. I'm going to continue to push forward. I'm going to continue to move. I'm going to continue to work hard and be persistent in my faith. It's only going to make the story even better because, one day, I will become a starter in the NFL."

I was so grateful for everything that they had sacrificed throughout all those years that I had been playing football. It was not a good feeling, but achieving greatness means staying committed to a dream.

Never stop believing in yourself. You are in full control of your actions at all times.

While you don't have control of people signing you, you are in control of whether you're going to have regrets or not. You also have control of being as ready as you possibly can be when that call comes. There's power in not giving up, in continuing to pursue your dreams, and believing in yourself.

CONCLUSION

I want to take a moment to sincerely thank everyone who has read this book. I truly believe that the stories and lessons shared within these pages will inspire you and provide the tools necessary to overcome the obstacles you face in your own life.

My hope is that the messages and experiences you've encountered here will resonate deeply with you. It's important to know that you are not alone in facing challenges—everyone has their own roadblocks. The key is to remain resilient, stay grounded, and keep your faith intact. Focus on what you can control, and you will find a way to overcome whatever stands in your path. Remember, persistence is power, and it's that relentless drive that will ultimately bring your dreams to fruition.

As you move forward, I encourage you to apply the lessons from my journey to your own life. For me, the next chapter is returning to the UFL in 2025. I'm excited to reconnect with a coaching staff that has always supported me and believes in my potential—especially Bob Stoops and Chuck Long. I truly believe this season will be a turning point, and I'm ready to contribute to a much stronger team.

Having just signed my contract, I'm fully committed to making this season count. I couldn't walk away from last season's results, and I'm determined to secure another championship with the Arlington Renegades. Stay tuned, because we'll be playing on major networks like Fox, ABC, and ESPN.

Thank you all for your support, and I hope to see you on the field!

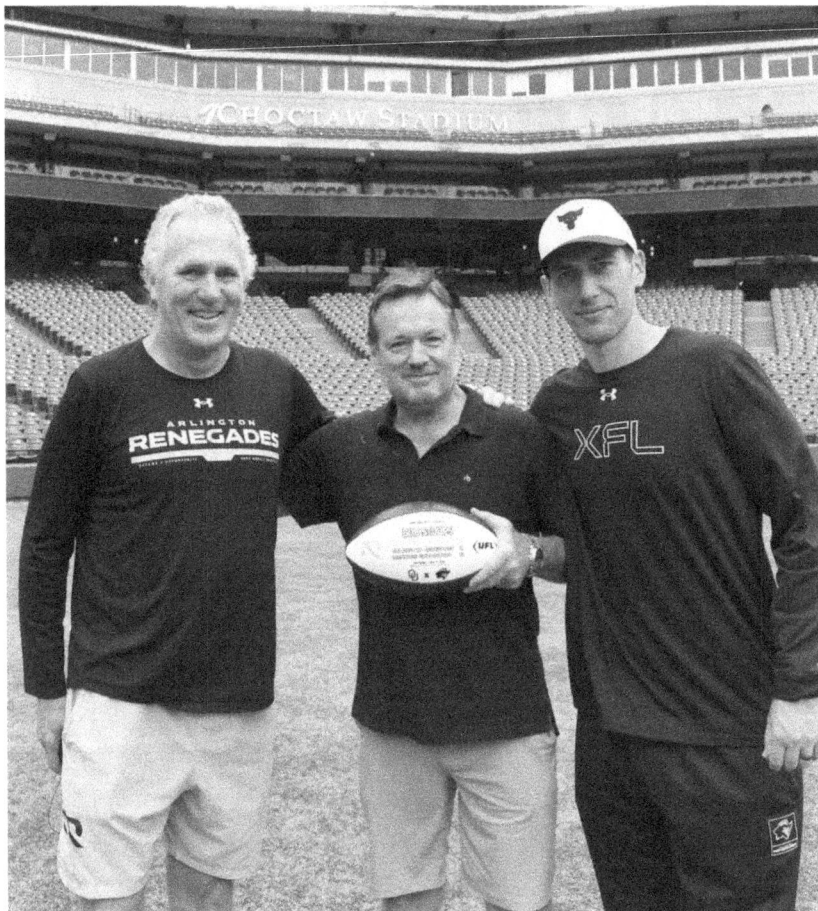

UFL Renegades Head Coach Bob Stoops and Offensive Coordinator Chuck Long.

I just want to take a moment to thank you for purchasing and reading a copy of my book—it really means a lot to me!

As a small token of my appreciation, I've got an exclusive bonus gift for you, designed to offer even more value and support.

Scan the QR Code:

I appreciate your interest in my book and value your feedback as it helps me improve future versions of this book. I would appreciate it if you could leave your invaluable review on Amazon.com with your feedback.
Thank you!

www.ingramcontent.com/pod-product-compliance
Lightning Source LLC
Chambersburg PA
CBHW021144090426
42740CB00008B/937